Jeremiah

LESSONS THROUGH THE STEPS OF
ONE OF GOD'S FAITHFUL SERVANTS

MANU SUSAN DAVID

Ark House Press
arkhousepress.com

© 2023 Manu Susan David

All rights reserved. Apart from any fair dealing for the purpose of study, research, criticism, or review, as permitted under the Copyright Act, no part may be reproduced by any process without written permission.

Unless otherwise stated, all Scriptures are taken from the New International Translation (Holy Bible. Copyright© 1996, 2004, 2007, 2013 by Tyndale House Foundation. Used by permission of Tyndale House Publishers Inc., Carol Stream, Illinois 60188. All rights reserved.)

Cataloguing in Publication Data:
Title: Jeremiah: Lessons through the steps of one of God's faithful servants
ISBN: 978-0-6458809-2-2 (pbk)
Subjects: REL074000 [RELIGION / Christian Ministry / Pastoral Resources]; REL012120 [RELIGION / Christian Living / Spiritual Growth]; REL006730 [RELIGION / Biblical Studies / Old Testament / Prophets];

Design by initiateagency.com

CONTENTS

Introduction			iii
1.	Let God be your Fuel and Fire	Jeremiah 1	1
2.	God, your Glory?	Jeremiah 2	7
3.	What Kind of Worship?	Jeremiah 7	13
4.	Run with Perseverance and Race with Endurance	Jeremiah 12:1-13	20
5.	Bound to God	Jeremiah 13:1-11	27
6.	Wander or Yield	Jeremiah 14	35
7.	In the Depths of Discouragement	Jeremiah 15	42
8.	Where our Hope is Found	Jeremiah 16	49
9.	Commit your Cause to God	Jeremiah 20	57
10.	Two Baskets of Figs	Jeremiah 24	63
11.	Truth or Falsehood	Jeremiah 28	68
12.	A Heart of Obedience	Jeremiah 35	74
13.	Consistent Communion with God	Jeremiah 36-39	80
14.	Trustworthy Father	Jeremiah 39:5-18 and 40:1-6	86
15.	Willing to do God's Will	Jeremiah 42 and 43	92
16.	Misplaced Trust	Jeremiah 44	98
17.	Being Faithful in a Fragmented World	Jeremiah 45	103
18.	The Narrow Path	Jeremiah 46-52	109

INTRODUCTION

Jeremiah was born and raised in Anathoth, a small town a few miles northeast of Jerusalem. The people of Judah had forsaken God by worshipping false gods *(Jeremiah 2:8; 7:9; 11:13)* and even went as far as building altars to Baal in order to burn their children as offerings *(Jeremiah 19:4-5)*. It is against this backdrop that God called Jeremiah to be a prophet to deliver his message to Judah (before, during and after its fall to Babylon in 586 B.C.). These prophecies included messages of warning and hope. He began his ministry around 627 BC and it ended sometime around 582 BC. The southern kingdom of Judah fell during Jeremiah's prophetic ministry (586 BC), having been threatened for many years by outside powers, first Assyria and Egypt and then by their eventual conquerors, Babylon.

Jeremiah addresses the people's sin and warned of the consequences of continuing in their sinful ways, that God would withdraw his hand from them *(Jeremiah 16:5-10)*. The nation would face famine and starvation. Invaders would plunder them; and they would be taken captive by a foreign power. But rather than respond with humility and repentance, the people of Judah continued in their ways and disregarded God's words of warning to them. Jeremiah witnesses the fulfillment of God's righteous judgement, and he shares in the sorrow and troubles that follow the destruction of Jerusalem.

The theme of Jeremiah can cause the book to feel heavy to study. But amidst the warnings of destruction, we find promises of hope, hope found not merely in the possibility of human repentance, but grounded squarely in the amazing grace of God.

The fall of Jerusalem came nearly nine hundred years after the original covenant between God and the Israelites in the Sinai desert *(Exodus 24:1-18)*. Such an extended period witnesses to God's great patience and mercy, allowing his people the opportunity to turn from their sinful ways. Although God is patient and merciful, there came a time when the people were answerable for their actions. It is important to delve deep into scripture on both aspects of this truth of God's character.

This study book takes the reader through the book of Jeremiah in a structured manner making 18 pitstops. The book delves into scripture on two aspects of the truth of God's character, a loving, merciful God and a Holy and just God who holds our actions to account. In addition, the book offers a unique insight into the mind and heart of one of God's faithful servants. Through the book, Jeremiah's emotional engagement, his compassion for people, frustrations with what God was calling him to do, the hostility he faced, his struggle with desiring judgment for those who did evil, and concern about his own safety is made evident. The book creates a connection between all these aspects and the reader's own spiritual journey.

To get a good grasp of these 18 lessons, it would be helpful to read through the book of Jeremiah as you do this study.

It is my prayer that you will be richly blessed as you work through this study.

LESSON 1

Let God be your Fuel and Fire

Fear of man will prove to be a snare
Provers 29:2

 Scripture Passage: ***Jeremiah 1***

When God speaks and lays out a plan for you that is profound, clear and specific, how would you respond? Would you feel thoroughly equipped, emboldened and well positioned to step into the role, even if it feels scary, and carry out the task God has laid out for you, or would you hesitate?

Jeremiah had a similar conundrum, God spoke and called Jeremiah for what he had planned and purposed for him.

The word of the Lord came to Jeremiah saying, *"Before I formed you in the womb, I knew you, before you were born, I set you apart; I appointed you as a prophet to the nations." (Jer 1:2)*

When God called Jeremiah, he was a young man, but God mentions that the call on his life was intentional from when he was in the womb.

God's words were not just to garner his attention but for him to understand that God had a specific purpose and plan for his life.

Self – Reflection: God creates each of us with intention and purpose. Has he been calling you to step into what he has purposed for you? The call may not be as direct as Jeremiah experienced, but he always intends for us to be instrumental in his kingdom purposes. Wherever he has placed you, ask God to reveal and lead you into what he has planned and purposed for you.

How does Jeremiah respond?

Jeremiah does not leap at the opportunity; his initial response is to hesitate and offer up an excuse. He says, *"I do not know how to speak; I am only a child." (Jer 1:6)*

How does God respond to Jeremiah?

He says *"Do not say, I am only a child. You must go to everyone I send you to and say whatever I command you. Do not be afraid of them for I am with you and will rescue you, declares the Lord." (Jer 1:7-8)*

Although Jeremiah offers up an excuse of not being able to speak, God knew what lay in his heart. He understood the underlying reason for Jeremiah's hesitation and that it stemmed from a place of fear.

Why was Jeremiah afraid?

The people of Judah were far removed from God in how they lived. And God's word to them was to repent and change their ways, otherwise they would be on the receiving end of God's righteous judgement. Jeremiah knew that such a message would not necessarily be welcome and hence the hesitation and fear to take on the role of prophet. Jeremiah was not only to speak to the common man of Judah, but he was to take God's message to the kings, officials and the priests. He knew that he would be met with hostility and opposition. Not the easiest of situations or position to be stepping into and hence the trepidation.

God Understands

When God responds to Jeremiah's excuse, he speaks words of comfort and reassurance. And he promises his presence would always be with Jeremiah and also assures him with the promise of rescue. Notice that God does not promise Jeremiah that he would never face trouble as his prophet. God's presence did not ensure absence of challenges but would ensure that he could withstand the trials he would face.

Self-Reflection: For you and me, that is the promise we can hold onto. The promise of his presence through all seasons of our lives, through the trials, the doubts, the fears and through any tough road that we have to walk through. Are you travelling the road of a difficult relationship, financial challenges, health issues, a trying work environment, an addiction, or a past trauma? Whatever it is, know that you are never alone, God's presence and power is with you through it all.

The way God responds to Jeremiah, teaches us that 'A lack of experience does not disqualify when God calls. He equips and sustains those he calls.' It is often our inexperience and incapabilities that drive us to humbly depend on God to accomplish what he has set out for us.

As God reassures Jeremiah, he also emphasises that all he wanted of Jeremiah was to be precise with what God instructs and he could not be selective in who he spoke to. Obedience in its entirety is what we see God wanting from Jeremiah. And he expects the same from us too.

Speaking or living out God's word cannot be governed by what is more palatable to hear or do. Or only spoken to those who seem more inclined to listen. But we are also to remember that what is spoken should be spirit led such that it would be what the people and culture need at that time and place.

💭 *Self-Reflection:* How often do we tend to respond like Jeremiah with doubt and fear? How often do we allow fear to chart a course for us, to drive our decisions and actions? We have to remember to be cautious in not tying wanting to do God's work with how we feel or if it would be successful in our eyes. The only measure is if it is in alignment with what God is asking of us.

Proverbs 29:25 *"Fear of man will prove to be a snare."*

Let's look at a couple of instances from scripture where this verse above proved to be true.

1 Samuel 15:24 King Saul says to Samuel, *"I have sinned. I violated the Lord's command and your instructions. I was afraid of the people and so I gave in to them."*

King Saul was instructed by Samuel who had a message from God to attack the Amalekites. This was punishment for the Amalekites from God for what they did to the people of God. God's word was very clear when he says to destroy them and all their possessions too.

But Saul does not heed the word of God entirely, he attacked the Amalekites, as we read in **1 Samuel 15:9** *"But Saul and his army spared king Agag and the best of the sheep and the cattle, the fat calves and lambs-everything that was good. These they were unwilling to destroy completely, but everything that was despised and weak, they totally destroyed."*

This act of disobedience by Saul grieves God and leads God to turn His hand and favour away from Saul. Saul chose to keep that which would please his men above God's will. The fear of not being favoured or popular among his men indeed proved to be a snare for him, it led him down a path of disobedience to God.

John 12:42-43 *"Yet at the same time many even among the leaders believed in Him (Jesus). But because of the Pharisees, they would not confess their faith for fear they would be put out of the synagogue; for they loved praise from men more than praise from God."*

Jesus taught and performed many miracles; this led some who were leaders among the Jews to believe in Him and yet they did not acknowledge it outwardly for the fear of others. For fear that they would not belong.

"For they loved the praise from men more than praise from God" – may we reflect and question if we allow that to be true in anything we do.

One of the truths that we glean from this initial phase of Jeremiah's life is that we are not to use either our environment or our perceived inability as an excuse to not follow what God calls us to do.

After the initial hesitation, Jeremiah obeyed God and was a prophet to the nations, his path was not trouble free, in fact Jeremiah did face a lot of hostility but God honoured his promise to Jeremiah by being with him through it all.

Prayer: We praise you God for all you have purposed and enabled us to be. When you call us to step out in faith, may our response to you not be riddled with doubt and fuelled by fear. May the fear of man not direct our path, or the praise of man be not what we seek or regard. But like a humble servant and child of God be obedient to your will and word. May we step out in faith and step forth in your strength to what you are calling us to do. May you be our fuel and our fire. Amen.

Discussion Questions

1. How did God announce to Jeremiah that he was chosen as a prophet? And what was Jeremiah's assessment of his own abilities in relation to God's call?
2. Have you ever been chosen for a task that you felt totally unfit to carry out? Have you ever talked yourself out of it by emphasising your weaknesses?
3. If Jeremiah had refused to obey the Lord, would he have been as guilty as the people who were disobedient to God?
4. What difference can it make to know that God knew us and set us apart even before our birth? How would this speak into moments when we doubt God's will for our life?
5. How did God respond to Jeremiah's reservations?
6. What consequences did God mention if Jeremiah would not be obedient? How does that impact our willingness to obey when God speaks?
7. Although the people would oppose Jeremiah, how did God make it clear to Jeremiah that there was nothing to fear?

What can we do to put into perspective the fear of God and fear of people/consequences?

LESSON 2

God, your Glory?

When there is less of God in your life, you inadvertently make room for something else to take his place

 Scripture Passage: ***Jeremiah 2***

What is one thing you value most in your life? Is it family, your job, your influence, or your earnings? Amongst all the things that the world we live in demands us to pay attention, where does God fit in?

In Jeremiah chapter 2, God calls himself the glory of his people. What does it mean for God to be our glory?

This passage begins with a recount of Israel's early relationship with God as evidenced by her devotion and willingness to follow him anywhere, even in the wilderness. But their devotion shifted and God questions, *what wrong did your fathers find in me?* There was no fault to be found in him, and yet the people went after other gods. In verse 5 God says, *"my people went after worthlessness and became worthless".*

As we work through this passage, the theme that stands out is Israel's faithlessness. But despite the multitude of sins and the stubbornness of the Israelites, God still calls them '*my people*'. Despite their behaviour, his desire was to draw them back to him and restore their relationship.

Self-Reflection: God's heart is always for us. He is our heavenly Father who made a way for us to be reconciled to him through the blood of his son Jesus. His heart yearns for each one of us to be restored to him. And in light of that truth, we always have hope. If you are praying for a loved one who is yet to correct their ways and turn to the Lord, know that it is the Lord's greatest desire for his children to be reconciled to him. Don't let the enemy's whispered lies take hold and diminish your hope. Keep praying and believing, the Lord does not give up and neither should we. Our hope is rooted not in our efforts or anyone else's but in who God is.

Jeremiah 2:11, *"Has a nation ever changed its gods? (yet they are not gods at all). But my people have exchanged their Glory for worthless idols."*
God calls himself 'The glory of his people'.
In **1 Samuel 15:29,** God is described as the Glory of Israel *"He who is the Glory of Israel does not lie or change His mind."*
Luke 2:32 *"The Lord is a light of revelation to the gentiles and the glory of your people Israel."*

Who are the people of God?

In *Genesis 12:2*, God says to Abraham *"I will make you into a great nation and I will bless you; I will make your name great, and you will be a blessing."* This nation becomes Israel, and they were recognised as the people of God. So, are any others considered people of God? Yes, Jesus came for each and every one of us and those that put their faith in him are his. Those that follow Him, who identify him as their Lord and saviour and those who belong to him through faith become part of the people of God.

Glory

The word glory in Hebrew **'Kobad'**, is used to describe the weight or heaviness of something. The more important something is, more is the glory ascribed to it. It is something that is impressive and demands recognition.

We often ascribe glory to God. He is worthy of it, glory radiates from God. It is the beauty of his Spirit. It is who he is, his nature and character. It is his infinite worth. God's glory has been described as his manifested presence, and also as the weightiness of his qualities such as his might, beauty, goodness, justice, love, grace and honour. This does not completely encompass his glory, as we with our finite minds cannot entirely comprehend it. God made everything to reveal his glory, all of nature exhibits his glory *"the heavens declare his glory* **(Psalm 19:1-4)**. All of his actions on earth reveal his glory. His glory was revealed to us in Jesus, **John 1:14** *says "The Word became flesh and made his dwelling among us. We have seen his glory, the glory of the one and only Son, who came from the Father, full of grace and truth."*

When we look at God being described as the 'Glory of his people', what does that mean for us? Do we as his people view him as our glory?

What/who is your glory?

What in your life holds the weight of being the most important thing to which glory (praise and honour) is ascribed?

Isaiah 43:7 *"everyone who is called by my name, whom I created for my glory, whom I formed and made."*

Yes, we are created for his glory – our ways, our walk and our words are to bring him glory. That is our purpose but how can we do that well if we do not primarily identify with the fact that he is our glory, that he should be the cause for any of our praise, the most magnificent part of our life, the reason for every honour.

- What are we recognised by in our time here? Is it intelligence, fame, power, beauty, prestige, wealth or a life lived for God?
- Where do we find our worth or weight in – is it that which is in the temporary or that which is eternal?

When we reflect on the above two questions it makes us realise that *'What we choose to find our worth in is what we end up dedicating most of time and energy to."* In the hustle of making it in today's world, how are we faring in keeping God pre-eminent with our time and with what we prioritise?

When God calls himself the glory of my people, he wants that to be a reality for each one of us who call ourselves followers of him.

The spirit in us will enable us to live in a manner that shapes us to be more like Christ every day, is that what we desire too? We have the knowledge that we should live a life pleasing to God but do the desires of the flesh and temptations of the world snuff out that desire before it becomes intended action. Are our desires aligned with that of God? Or like the verse in Jeremiah says, do we exchange God for worthless idols?

Our glory, when not found to be God, but in things of the flesh, result in us not giving God his due place in our lives. And when there is less of God in our lives, we inadvertently make room for something else to take his place. God says that he is the glory of his people, but ultimately it is a choice for us to ensure that it remains a lived-out reality every single day of our lives.

Prayer: May you alone Lord, be the centre point around which everything else finds its position and place. May you be the most magnificent part of our lives, and may you be our glory, the one who is ascribed a place of pre-eminence in our lives, the one who holds the most weight in the why and how of everything we do. Amen.

Discussion Questions

1. What do you think led the people to forsake God for other gods? How might we see that happen today?
2. How would you define glory?
3. What does living for God's glory mean to you? What might hinder us from giving God his due glory?
4. Share your thoughts on God calling himself the glory of his people?

How would you tie the two concepts together, that he created us for his glory and that He is our Glory?

LESSON 3

What kind of Worship?

Worship should be an overflow of our heartfelt devotion to God

 Scripture Passage: *Jeremiah 7*

Jeremiah 7:2 *"Stand at the gate of the Lord's house and there proclaim this message. Hear the word of the Lord, all you people of Judah who come through these gates to worship the Lord."*

These words spoken from the gates of the temple was from God through Jeremiah directed at the people who were still actively engaged in worship in the Lord's temple.

The temple was central to the people, and it was a significant part of their lives. It was characterized by beauty both on the outside as well as on the inside. The temple had pure bronze columns, golden incense altars and lamp stands, wooden cherubim, each ten feet tall with outstretched wings. Inside the holy place, and in the innermost part of the temple, was the Ark of the Covenant, signifying the very presence of God.

The Israelites although far removed from being devoted to God, continued to diligently carry on their rituals in the temple. They seem to have deceived themselves into thinking that repeating religious words and following religious rituals when they were at the temple in Jerusalem was all that was needed to be right with God.

To obey is better than sacrifice

God sees our hearts. The people's worship was not an overflow of their heartfelt devotion to God and nor did it pour out into other aspects of their lives. God wanted them to reform their ways, in verse 3 God says, *"Reform your ways and your actions and I will let you live in this place."*

What were the people doing that they had to change their ways? In verses 5-9 we get an insight into their actions that were displeasing to God.

- Injustice
- Oppression
- Murder
- Idolatry
- Stealing
- Adultery

God warns them, *"Do not to listen to deceptive words and say, this is the temple of the Lord, the temple of the Lord, the temple of the Lord."* (Jer 7:4)

The people were given a false sense of being right with God by the false prophets in that they were made to believe that by performing rituals at the temple, they could appease God and thereby be exempt from God's judgement. The meaningless and repetitive mention of the words *'this is the Lord's temple'* is not what God was seeking after but genuine worship and a change of heart. We read similar words in **Matthew 7:21** where Jesus says, *"Not everyone who says to me, Lord, Lord will enter the Kingdom of heaven, but only he who does the will of my Father in heaven."*

The people seemed to give more emphasis and value to the temple than to God, forgetting that it is God's presence that makes the temple significant in worship.

In verse 10, God says that after committing all the above-mentioned sins, *"They come and stand before me in this house, which bears my name and say, we are safe"– safe to do all these detestable things?"*

Picture carrying on living without a sense of God's moral standard then rushing back to God, confessing, and asking for forgiveness and then reverting back to living outside the standard God sets for us. **James 2:20** says *"Faith without deeds is useless."* And **1 Samuel 15:22** says, to obey is better than sacrifice.

God is far more interested in our heart's condition, in how we treat each other than in any religious act one can perform, because the presence of God is not meant to leave one unchanged but instead transform.

Do we see parallels today with this sort of worship?

The Israelites relied on the presence of the temple, thinking if they followed their rituals all was good between them and God. Just like going to the temple did not make them faithful, going to church on Sunday does not define one's faithfulness. God knows and God sees. God doesn't just want to be a part of our Sunday. God wants us and our whole life. Worship is not attached to a place or a church, but our lives are meant to be a form of worship to God. Worship at church that does not reflect a life given to and lived for God but instead is an obligatory practice is not what God desires from us. The question we need to ask ourselves is, where is the following of Christ in that sort of a life? God is not in the business of redeeming buildings; he is for redeeming people. He is not after offerings but the changed hearts of people.

God desired for the Israelites to change their ways. God says, *"If you change your ways, then I will let you live in this place." (Jer 7:3, 7)*

What place is God talking about? In verse 7 we read, *"In the land that I gave your forefathers forever and ever."* The land that they were living in was theirs, given by God and God himself reminds them that it is theirs forever. That gift was God's blessing and provision to them, but their acts of disobedience and rebellion put them in a position where they were going to be removed from that blessing and promise.

We saw that happen with the Israelites, after being led out of Egypt by God through Moses. They rebelled and disobeyed God and an entire generation did not get to set foot in the promised land *(Deuteronomy 1:35)*.

Our choices and actions always do have consequences. God is a loving and forgiving Father but he who bestows everything so lavishly on us clearly states that in response to his love and grace, an intentional effort and desire to walk in a manner that honours him and is pleasing to him is necessitated.

Jeremiah 7:11*"Has this house which bears my Name become a den of robbers to you?* We see this verse quoted by Jesus in **Matthew 21:13** when he enters the temple and chases out all those who were buying and selling.

When we gather for worship in God's name – what are we making that place out to be – a house of prayer, a beacon of hope, a place for lost and weary souls, a place that reflects Christ's love, compassion, forgiveness, and acceptance, or do we make it a den of robbers? Robbing people of the chance to know Christ by twisting the design and purpose that God had for what church should be?

WHAT KIND OF WORSHIP?

God's heart

Jeremiah 7:13 *"While you were doing all these things, declares the Lord, I spoke to you again and again, but you did not listen; I called you, but you did not answer."*

We see God's faithfulness to his people here. While they lived displeasing him, he called and spoke to them again and again. A heart full of love who does not give up on his people, persistent in drawing them back to him is what we see here. The Lord spoke and he called, but the Israelites chose not to listen and did not respond to his call.

Self-Reflection: Is God speaking to you today about something he wants you to let go off? Is he calling you to a deeper walk of faith with him or if you have not acknowledged him as your Lord, is he calling you to do so? The Lord was faithful then and he is faithful now. He wants us to draw close to him, partake in genuine heartfelt worship and have hearts that desire him and lives that reflect that reality. If we want to walk a life of faith with Him, we need to reflect on our actions and the path we are on and then correct our trajectory to ensure that the guiding light in all we do is always him.

God then tells Jeremiah not to pray for the people (*Jer 7:16*). Prayer is a vital part of our relationship with God, he calls us to pray. Even though he knows what we need, we are asked to take our petitions to him. After seeing God's repeated calls for the people to turn back to him, why does he want Jeremiah to stop praying for them? Shouldn't praying for the people be more urgent considering they were being stubborn towards God.

How do you reconcile God asking Jeremiah not to pray for the people?

God uses his judgement here to jar people out of their disobedience, to break that stubborn set of hearts and soften them towards Him. When repeated words of warning are not heeded, tough times can serve to cause one to reflect and realise the error of one's ways. Difficult and challenging moments can push one to shift focus from self to God. Do you tend to turn to God only when there is no other door left to knock on?

Prayer: Thank you Lord for being so patient with us when we falter. May our lives be one of worship to you, heeding your voice and walking in all the ways you command us and may we heed your voice of correction and honour you with our obedience. Amen.

WHAT KIND OF WORSHIP?

 Discussion Questions

1. How would you describe the spiritual condition of the people, even though they were going to the temple and offering sacrifices?
2. What were the Lord's words to those who were coming to the temple? What was the promise if they would amend their ways?
3. What are some of the false securities that we can rest on when it comes to feeling right with God?
4. Was Jeremiah condemning the sacrificial system? Reading Jeremiah 7:21-24, what matters to God more?
5. In Verse 11, we read *"Has this house which bears my Name become a den of robbers to you?,* also said by Jesus in *Matthew 21:13,* What scenarios in today's church might compel the same words to come from Jesus?
6. Discuss your thoughts about God telling Jeremiah not to pray for the people? (v16)

When praying for a loved one, discuss your thoughts on praying with the perspective of either consequences to be removed or for them to turn back to God through those consequences?

LESSON 4

Run with Perseverance and Race with Endurance

In the Lord we are Overcomers and Victorious

 Scripture Passage: ***Jeremiah 12:1-13***

Jeremiah 12: 5 *"If you have raced with men on foot and they have worn you out, how can you compete with horses? If you stumble in safe country, how will you manage in the thickets by the Jordan?*

It was through Jeremiah that God sends words of warning to the Israelites, to change their ways and right themselves with God. And if they did not heed those cautionary words, they would face God's punishment. In Jeremiah 2 we learnt about Israel forsaking God, who said, *"My people have committed two sins: They have forsaken me, the spring of living water, and have dug their own cisterns (idols), broken cisterns that cannot hold water."(Jer 2:13)*

The Israelites do not take to heart Jeremiah's cautionary words but instead continue sinning and the prophet is subjected to endure hardship at their hands as a result of the message he was bringing forth. In Jeremiah chapter 12 we see him share his frustration of how the wicked seem not only to be spared but also flourishing *(grow and bear fruit, verse 2)*, while Jeremiah seems to be going through various challenges as he stays obedient to God, doing what God calls him to.

Jeremiah airs his complaint to God.

Jeremiah 12:1b *"Why do the wicked prosper? And why do the faithless live at ease?*

Jeremiah, at this point seems to be struggling to understand God's ways and his timing. Through the prophet's words in this passage, we get a glimpse into the thoughts he was struggling with. He wanted God to hasten up his judgement on the disobedient people and could not comprehend why God seemed to allow them to prosper while he suffered at their hands.

Self- Reflection: Have you ever felt similarly, i.e., poured your heart out to God wondering why he allows for those who seem to be doing wrong to live at ease while you struggle through challenges while striving to be obedient to him?

Scripture reminds us that those who sin and go against God will be held accountable for their actions.

Romans 2:6 *"God will give to each person according to what he has done."*

Romans 2:8 *"For those who are self-seeking and who reject the truth and follow evil, there will be wrath and anger."*

God's justice, love and mercy are all perfectly balanced. His justice is imminent but his love and mercy and the desire for people to turn to him is also prominent and only God can perfectly execute all these in his own timing.

God's delay in judgement was frustrating for Jeremiah, but that delay, was a glimpse into the heart of a merciful God, giving time and opportunity for people to repent and turn to him. And remember that although Jeremiah had challenges, he also had God's protection as was promised to him in *Jeremiah 1:18* *"Today I have made you a fortified city, an iron pillar and a bronze wall- against the kings of Judah, the officials, the priests and the people. They will fight against you but will not overcome for I am with you and will rescue you."*

Self-Reflection: Take a moment and think about God's patience with us. If God was not patient with us and was quick to mete out justice for our wrongs, where would we be? He does not give up on us and extends that same grace to those who are yet to give their heart to him. We will not comprehend all aspects of why God does something, or his timing, after all, the ways of God are beyond what we can fathom. But as we spend time in his word and in prayer, we do grow in our understanding of him and it enables us to trust him at all moments including the times that do not make sense to our finite minds.

When Jeremiah felt a dip in his unwavering trust in God's ways and his heart began to fill with 'why' questions of his own, rather than turn away from God when doubts assailed, he took that as an opportunity to turn to God.

Self-Reflection: A very humbling reminder for us all. None of us are perfect and will have moments when we struggle with why God allows certain things to happen or why he seems not to respond promptly or in a manner that we expect. It is especially in those moments that we must turn to God and take what is in our hearts to him. God loves and cares for us and will meet us where we are at. In addition, turning to him helps us rest our focus on him through our tough moments and keeps us from steering away from God and helps build our faith in those times.

Check my heart, God

Even though Jeremiah was struggling to understand God's ways, he lays out his heart to him in a very honest way, airing his frustrations and asking God to punish the people, Jeremiah prays to God and asks God to check his heart.

Jeremiah 12:3 "*Yet you know me, O Lord; you see me and test my thoughts about you.*"

This prayer from the prophet is reflective of a heart that has spent time with God and in his word to know that God is righteous and faithful and one can never truly rely on one's own feelings to determine the goodness of God. And so, Jeremiah asks God to look into his thoughts, for however far removed from understanding God's ways he might have felt in that moment, he did not want that to lead him to be far removed from being under God's will.

Self-Reflection: Although Jeremiah's anger and frustration may feel justified on some levels to us, he reminds us to never entertain thoughts that goes against God's love, will and desire. Can we with confidence say that we respond in a similar manner?

How does God respond to Jeremiah?

God says, "*If you have raced with men on foot and they have worn you out, how can you compete with horses? If you stumble in safe country, how will you manage in the thickets by the Jordan?*" (Jer 12:5)

God uses two metaphors to help Jeremiah understand. In each of these metaphors, God points out that things would get tougher for Jeremiah. In the metaphors, initially the race is with men but later it is with horses, from walking in safe country you move onto the thickets in the Jordan. God's answer did not entail words of comfort or assurance of the removal of the issue, but instead pointed to the work he was doing within his prophet. God was building up Jeremiah in this season through these trials so he would be made stronger to stand firm to face what lies ahead.

Self-Reflection: We never want to go through our tough moments, but God allows those moments to build us up spiritually if there is a will and desire in us to surrender and be shaped by him. We know that times are not going to get easier for followers of Christ. The contention the world will have with us is not unexpected. If we stumble when things are easier, how would we know to trust and lean on God when times are difficult. How would we have the firmness in our faith to cling to God through it all. Jeremiah needed to learn how to trust God in these smaller challenges and be dependent on him so that he was more rooted in God to face more trying times. Similarly, we too need to remember that any trials we face is an opportunity where God can strengthen, shape and build our faith.

One of the metaphors God uses is competing with a horse in a race. Competing with a horse in a race seems like a sure loss and yet God talks about it. The impossibility of winning against a horse feels obvious to us, but what God is reminding Jeremiah and us is that challenges that come our way may seem impossible for us to overcome on our own but when God is with us, that impossibility becomes a possibility. And through him we are overcomers and victorious.

As followers of Christ, if we truly walk in the path of the Lord, we will encounter moments where we will feel like Jeremiah did, lonely, wronged and persecuted by others. At those times we may we look to God with some 'why' questions of our own. We might not have the answer to the 'why' for many questions, but we can rest with certainty that God is in control, that he is merciful, he desires for all to know him, he wants us to persevere, endure, grow in his strength and run our race with faithfulness and obedience to the very end. And through it all, he is right there with us building us up and incorporating us in his plans and purposes.

Prayer: Lord, when we have moments of frustration or doubt, may we turn to you with what is in our hearts. Grant us the strength to stay rooted in you Lord, to run our race with perseverance and endurance. Equip and carry us through the tests of today and the challenges of tomorrow so that we continue to shine your light in this world. Amen.

Discussion Questions

1. What was Jeremiah's complaint to the Lord?
2. Discuss your thoughts on understanding the concept of why the wicked prosper or why bad things happen to good people (What scripture passages you lean on to understand this)?
3. What can we learn about how Jeremiah dealt with the frustration he felt and with the challenging questions he had?
4. What do we glean about God's character through this passage?
5. What was God's response to Jeremiah's complaint? Discuss your thoughts about it?

LESSON 5

Bound to God

Rest in the knowledge that we are his and let it be known as the reason for all we do

 Scripture Passage: *Jeremiah 13:1-11*

Proverbs 16:18 *"Pride goes before destruction, a haughty spirit before a fall."*

Although Jeremiah consistently spoke God's words of warning to the Israelites, their leaders persisted in their idolatry and the assimilation of sinful practices of the wicked nations around them to such an extent that God was forced to deal severely with their unfaithfulness. They lacked the discernment and humility to understand the wrong they were doing and were stubborn hearted towards God's call for them to repent.

In *Jeremiah 13:1-11*, we see God use the imagery of a linen belt and demonstrated to Jeremiah that if the people continued to rebel against him with no sign of repentance, he will ruin the ***pride*** of Judah and the great ***pride*** of Jerusalem.

God's intent was not the ruin of the people, it was the ruin of their sin, which was pride. Sinful pride is described as *'the belief in one's own abilities and achievements where recognition of God's sovereignty and grace is absent.*

Scripture constantly warns us of the sin of pride; Pride was what led to the downfall of Lucifer (Satan) *(Ezekiel 28:17, "Your heart became proud on account of your beauty, and you corrupted your wisdom because of your splendour. So, I threw you to the earth; I made a spectacle of you before kings").* Despite the fact that God had created Satan and gave him all of the power and beauty he possessed, Satan wanted all of the glory. He turned into the enemy of God when he chose not to worship God in response to the gifts he was given.

Self-Reflection: When we tend to place ourselves or anything else before our creator, it is the pride deep down within us that holds us back from submitting to him. Anything that dethrones God from his rightful position within our hearts and takes his place is definitely an issue. Rebellion toward God is often manifested as resistance to his word. We see that with the Israelites here, deep down, pride hardened their hearts towards God's words. It is always important to ask God to check our hearts and reveal any pride. And when he does, surrender it to him and ask him to help you submit to him. God desires for us to come to him with anything and everything. Being close to God helps us remain sensitive to the wrong in our lives.

God speaks

In this passage, God speaks to Jeremiah four times. God ***directs*** Jeremiah step by step in the mission that is entrusted to him.

💭 *Self-Reflection:* He is a God who speaks. Are we listening to the voice of God like how Jeremiah did? God desires to speak to us and communicates with us through different ways; Are we taking the time to listen? He directs us every step of the way; Do we pay heed or march on to our own thoughts and wisdom? Take a moment and reflect if your time with God is mainly you talking to God or are you intentional with wanting to listen to what he is saying to you.

Jeremiah's Obedience

In this passage, Jeremiah embodies an obedience that is not based on knowing all the answers prior to obeying what God asked of him. As God directed Jeremiah, he does not give clarity initially to the why of his directive, but that did not put a pause on Jeremiah's obedience. God directed him in steps, without laying out the entire plan.

💭 *Self-Reflection:* Similar to how God directed Jeremiah one step at a time without laying out the entirety of what Jeremiah had to do or the 'why' behind what he was doing, God often works the same way in our lives too. He nudges us and directs us one step at a time and wants us to trust him enough to take those initial steps. But fear and uncertainty can prevent us from following through. It is human nature to want the entire plan to be laid out before we take that first step. Jeremiah's obedience is a humbling reminder for us to take steps with faith in obedience, trusting our Sovereign God and Heavenly Father.

God directed Jeremiah to buy a Linen belt, wear it, then hide it and eventually dig it out *(verses 1-6)*.

We will look at the **four action words** here that Jeremiah followed and allow that to speak into being obedient and listening to God (as Jeremiah did).

Bought – God instructed Jeremiah to buy a linen belt. A linen belt was a priestly garment. As per God's instruction, buying the belt, would have cost Jeremiah a certain amount.

Self-Reflection: At times, following God's leading and being obedient to him will cost us. It can cost us our time, our comfort, our convenience, our resources, certain relationships or even some friendships. Reflect on what you are willing to give up, so as to be and stay obedient to God?

Wore – Jeremiah had to wear the linen belt till God told him otherwise.

Self-Reflection: There are times when being obedient to God will require us to embody the word. Times when we have to ensure that our faith is known as the reason why we make certain choices – to not gossip, to be morally fair and right, to treat everyone equally. Our faith is not something we go yelling out on the streets about, but like the linen belt, when worn, it is part of who we are – and that is how we must embody our faith.

Hid – Jeremiah was told to take off the linen belt and hide it in a crevice

Psalm 119:11 says *"I have hidden your word in my heart so that I may not sin against you."* Meditate and hide his words and his promises deep within your hearts.

Self-Reflection: It is important and necessary to make time for God, read scripture, pray, and store God's word in our heart and in our mind, so that it stays with us and will give us comfort in moments when we need it, provide strength to be obedient through difficult circumstances, and will enables us to reflect Christ to others when otherwise we might lean toward reacting in the flesh.

Dug – Jeremiah was to dig out the linen belt after a certain time when God instructs him to. Digging takes some effort. If you have ever tried digging a hole for any DIY garden project, let me tell you, it is hard, hard work.

Self-Reflection: There are times when being obedient to God will require more effort than we expect on our part for the word of God to be revealed to those around us. Being there for someone, acts of help, kindness, forgiveness, love and compassion are not the easiest things to carry out but often they help us show someone, Christ's love.

Take some time and reflect on the four questions that challenged me as I spent time in this passage.

- Following God will cost us something, if it is not, then are we missing the mark in following him wholeheartedly?
- Do we wear our faith with confidence and allow it to affect our choices?
- Do we hide his word in our hearts and allow it to build us up and strengthen us?
- Are we willing to put effort into doing the things the Lord has asked of us or do we say it is too hard and give up?

The belt symbolised how Israel and Judah were bound to God by Him, *"For as a belt is bound around the waist, so I bound all the people of Israel and all the people of Judah to me,' declares the Lord, 'to be my people for my renown and praise and honour. But they have not listened." (Jeremiah 13:11)*

For what purpose? – God says, to be **my people** for my **renown, praise** and **honour.**

The Lord had purposed for his people to be bound to him, bringing him Glory. But they became tarnished and polluted by surrounding influences.

Linen was a material worn by priests – **Leviticus 16:4** *"He is to put on the sacred linen tunic, with linen undergarments next to his body; he is to tie the linen sash around him and put on the linen turban. These are sacred garments; so, he must bathe himself with water before he puts them on."* And Israel was to be a priestly nation for the Lord – **Exodus 19:6** *"You will be for me a kingdom of priests and a holy nation.' These are the words you are to speak to the Israelites."*

When we accept Jesus as our saviour, he binds us to him. And our purpose is to glorify him in all that we do. We are to be his people – that should be our identity, and it should be what others recognize us by. When we focus on ourselves or the noise around us more than Jesus, listening to him gets difficult and doing what he says becomes almost impossible. We can't praise God when we are constantly praising ourselves.

What were the people's downfall?

- Pride – following the dictates of their own heart
- Serving other gods
- Refusing to hear God

The belt when worn – symbolised being bound to God and while being bound to him, we live in our true identity, we serve our purpose, we add to the glory of God and rest under his protection.

The belt when removed and is in the crevice in the rocks – As it says in verse 7 was eventually ruined and completely useless. When separated from God, the things of this world can surround, press upon us and influence us. We are separated from our refuge and our fortress. And without the wisdom, guidance and conviction of the Spirit, we lose what God designed and purposed us to be, and we can impart nothing towards his Kingdom purposes because without him we are nothing.

God binds us to him, but he invites us to play an active part in the relationship that we have with him. This will require a few definitive actions -

- Serve God and Worship him only – You shall have no other gods before me *(Exodus 20:3)*.
- Obedience – If you love me, keep my commandments *(John 14:15)*
- Humble ourselves - Humble yourselves before the Lord and he will lift you up *(James 4:10)*.

Prayer: May we like Jeremiah listen to the voice of God and trust him even if we do not know the why or what is to come. May we not allow pride to be our motivation but rather may all that we do, be for him and for his glory. May we rest in the knowledge that we are his and let it be known as the reason for all that we do. May we reflect on anything that we might prioritise before God, be it a relationship, self, work, entertainment or anything else. And when we falter Lord, may we humble ourselves, repent and turn to you. And may our actions, choices and the desires of our hearts not cause us to be separated from you Lord, but remain bound to you. Amen.

Discussion Questions

1. What was God's directive to Jeremiah?
2. What do you take away from how the directions were given to Jeremiah and his response to it?
3. What is the significance of the Linen belt?
4. What did you understand about each step and its meaning for the message God was trying to convey?
5. Share your thoughts on applying each of those directives (Bought, wearing, hide, dug up) to being obedient to God?
6. God wanted to ruin their sin. What was it? What do you think led the people to become so prideful?
7. What does God say about pride? (Look up verses or stories in scripture for this)

It is God who binds his people to him, what is our part in remaining bound to him?

LESSON 6

Wander or Yield

We all are inclined to wander if we are not purposeful in our pursuit of God

 Scripture Passage: **Jeremiah 14**

Jeremiah 14:10a *"This is what the Lord says about the people: They greatly love to wander; they do not restrain their feet."*

The people of Israel were complacent about their obedience to God. Their false prophets and priests were misleading the people to think that their continuous disobedience would not lead them to suffer any consequences *(Jeremiah 14:13, "But I said, "Alas, Sovereign Lord! The prophets keep telling them, 'You will not see the sword or suffer famine. Indeed, I will give you lasting peace in this place.").* And as a result, the people chose to ignore the words of warning from Jeremiah, carrying on in their disobedient ways, wandering further away from God instead of submitting to him.

As a nation when Israel rebelled against God and continued to be in a place of disobedience, they began to endure life removed from under the wing of God's provision and peace. They as a people found themselves in a place of spiritual as well as a physical drought as seen in *Jeremiah 14.*

Drought

The chapter begins with a vivid description of the drought the people of Israel were enduring. The passage is inundated with language that paints a very realistic picture of the situation then. Words such as mourn, languish, wail, cry, dismay, lack of rain, empty cisterns, dry ground and lack of pasture give us a glimpse of their reality at the time.

Drought was one of the punitive consequences of disobedience to the covenant as described in Leviticus and Deuteronomy.

Leviticus 26:19-20, "I will break down your stubborn pride and make the sky above you like iron and the ground beneath you like bronze. Your strength will be spent in vain, because your soil will not yield its crops, nor will the trees of your land yield their fruit.

Deuteronomy 28:22-24, "The Lord will strike you with wasting disease, with fever and inflammation, with scorching heat and drought, with blight and mildew, which will plague you until you perish. The sky over your head will be bronze, the ground beneath you iron. The Lord will turn the rain of your country into dust and powder; it will come down from the skies until you are destroyed."

Self-Reflection: We all are inclined to wander if we are not purposeful in our pursuit of God. It can begin with as a small shift, for example; a lack of diligence in our daily time with God which to begin with might occurs sporadically but gradually over time becomes more habitual and eventually can usher us to a place of spiritual drought. The absence of that ever-present intimacy with the Lord is when we experience a spiritual barrenness.

Staying connected to our source of living water, the well spring, from whom we need to drink from every day is imperative for a follower of Christ. When that vital connection to God is amiss, we are parched, dry in spirit, our soul mourns and our ground (works for God) is cracked, yielding nothing for the kingdom of God.

Jeremiah pleads on the people's behalf

Jeremiah calls upon the Lord to show mercy and offers a heartfelt prayer *"Although our sins testify against us, do something, Lord, for the sake of your name. For we have often rebelled; we have sinned against you. You who are the hope of Israel, its Saviour in times of distress, why are you like a stranger in the land, like a traveller who stays only a night? Why are you like a man taken by surprise, like a warrior powerless to save? You are among us, Lord, and we bear your name; do not forsake us! (Jer 14:7-9).*

Jeremiah grieves for the people and calls upon God to extend mercy. Jeremiah does not minimise their sin but understands what God has allowed is justified and yet he calls upon God to do something for HIS NAME.

God's name is his identity and reputation – that by which he is known. In **Ezekiel 20:9** we read *"For the sake of my name, I (God) did what would keep it from being profaned in the eyes of the nations they lived among and to whose sight I have revealed myself to the Israelites by bringing them out of Egypt."*

The verse above reveals to us that God did what was needed so that his name was not profaned. Jeremiah leans into God's mercy and love, pleading for the people who bear his name, and for his name's sake, that he may look upon the people with mercy.

💭 *Self-Reflection:* We as his people bear his name – as bearers of his name, how do we carry and represent that name out in the world? Are we cautious to not be the cause for anyone to profane the Lord's name?

Jeremiah calls God *'the people's hope and saviour'*, who is among them and will not forsake them. At all times, this is who is he is to us too. Turn to him with hope. However difficult a situation, God is and will always be our constant hope in whom we can trust. May we remember and let that truth fill our hearts.

Love to Wander

God says of the people to Jeremiah, they **love to wander** and they **do not restrain their feet**.

They love to wander – their hearts desire was not tied to do what is good, right and pleasing to God anymore. They seemed to find their joy in doing what they wished to.

💭 *Self-Reflection:* We often begin our spiritual journey with God letting go of things we might have once loved, but know that it would not be something God would want us to continue in. And as we continue to walk in obedience to him, we find that the desire to do that which is right in God's eyes only grows within us. When God describes the love for the people to wander away from him, it reflects the state of their heart and how far removed from the Almighty they truly were.

They wandered after false gods and did not restrain their feet. Not restraining their feet, reflects a lack of self-control in their choice to keep God first and foremost.

Self-Reflection: The enemy strikes us in many ways but the most effective is when his attempts are directed towards making our daily steps gradually turn away from God because it is then that we get spiritually weak. We, like the people of Israel also have a tendency to wander, to sin, be self-serving and grow complacent in our daily walk with God. It is imperative to recognise it and be intentional in our pursuit of God.

Keeping our feet upon Solid Ground

As a start, recognising that we all are prone to wander is important. Following that, it is also crucial to create habits in our daily lives that help guard against the slippery slope of wandering. Reading the word, praying, doing a group bible study, corporate worship and fellowship, all of these play a part in helping us stay the course.

In Psalms, we read time and time again David expressing that the Lord is his desire and it is HE who places his feet upon solid ground. It always begins with God; We do what we can but may we always lean on the Lord who enables and empowers us to diligently walk our spiritual path.

Psalm 40:2 says, *"He lifted me out of the slimy pit, out of the mud and mire; he set my feet on a rock and gave me a firm place to stand."*

It is God who keeps us steady on the path. In our own strength we will struggle. Turn to God and call upon his name and he will enable and empower us to walk diligently with him.

Psalm 66:9 says, *"He has preserved our lives and kept our feet from slipping."*

Yes, God holds us firm and keeps us strong and steady on our path but what do we have to do, to be able to receive that from him - Yield to him, wait on him and seek him.

Psalm 119:105 says *"Your word is a lamp unto my feet"*

His word guides our path, immerse yourself in his word for his word is powerful and it steers us towards God. Spend time in prayer not only speaking and laying all that is on our hearts to him but also waiting on him to listen to what he has to say.

Nicki Gumbel who pioneered the alpha course says, we don't go to the doctor, tell all that is bothering us and then just walk out. No, we wait to hear what the doctor has to say and heed his advice. In the same way, take time to wait and listen to what God has to say.

Wandering is so much easier in the moment than yielding to God. It is vital to remember that there is a cumulative consequence to our desires, choices and the daily decisions and actions we make that either honour God or not.

Prayer: May the desires of our heart be aligned with God; may we yield to him and seek him every day so that we can be strong and steady in our daily walk with God. May God give us the strength to restrain our feet from wandering and may we find peace and joy as we submit to him, for he is our hope and our saviour. Amen.

Discussion Questions

1. How are the conditions in drought-stricken Judah described? How was drought connected to the covenant?
2. Drawing a parallel between the physical and spiritual drought the people of Judah were in, what is 'Spiritual drought', what can lead us into it and how can we navigate through it?
3. What was Jeremiah's plea to God? (v7-9) and how does God answer him? (v10-11).
4. Discuss guard rails we can place in our lives that can prevent us from wandering?
5. How does Jeremiah further try to reason with God? (14:13) Who does God say will be punished? (v14-16).

Read *Deuteronomy 18:20, 2 Peter 2:1, 2 Corinthians 11:13-15, Matthew 15:14, James 3:1-2* and discuss the insight scripture gives about how false teachers/prophets will be dealt with?

LESSON 7

In the Depths of Discouragement

"They shall fight against you, but they shall not prevail, for I am with you."
Jeremiah 15:20

  Scripture Passage: *Jeremiah 15*

Jeremiah continues to bring God's word to the people, confronting them about their sin, warning them about God's judgement that would come upon them unless they repent and turn from their ways. The people, stubborn in their ways and in their hearts, not only ignored God's words, but also mocked, scorned and persecuted God's messenger, Jeremiah. As we read through Jeremiah chapter 15, we see discouragement pour out from the prophet throughout the chapter. His cries to God reveal his feelings on the unfair treatment he receives from the people even though he has done no wrong towards them.

IN THE DEPTHS OF DISCOURAGEMENT

The prayer of a discouraged servant

Jeremiah 15:15 *"You **understand** O lord, remember me and care for me. **Avenge me** on my persecutors. You are **long-suffering** -do not take me away, think of how I suffer reproach for your sake."* (emphasis mine)

Jeremiah is burdened and overwhelmed. What does he do when he feels like that? He takes his heavy heart including his emotions to God in prayer, and says "You understand O lord." And then asks God to act on his behalf by avenging the wrong done to him.

Self-Reflection: Yes, the Lord does understand, what a comfort to know that we can go to God in prayer with all that is in our hearts, even our raw emotions and know that he can truly understand our pain and our plight.

As Jeremiah pleads with God, he asks God to avenge those who persecute him. How often do we long for God to put into place those that make life difficult for us? Although we often wish to see some sort of retribution to those who do no good to us, God's focus is beyond the temporary to the eternal. Jeremiah calls God as long-suffering here, Jeremiah knows that God is patient with the people, giving them time to change their ways, because he is a God who loves and desires for all to turn to him. God's long-suffering nature reveals God's love, mercy and patience even in the midst of the people's disobedience.

Jeremiah continues speaking to God saying, *"When your words came to me, I ate them; they were my joy and my heart's delight, for I bear your name, O lord God Almighty." (Jeremiah 15:16)*

Jeremiah trusted in God and delighted in his word, but that did not mean the path he had to take was easy or his troubles spontaneously disappeared. There were times when the pain was all too much for Jeremiah.

Jeremiah 15:18 *"Why is my pain unending and my wound grievous and incurable? Will you be to me like a deceptive brook, like a spring that fails?"*

This verse is filled with the heaviness of Jeremiah's discouragement and despair. And he questions God in the process. In Jeremiah 2:13, God tells Jeremiah that one of the sins of the people was that they have forsaken HIM- **the spring of living water.** And although Jeremiah believed him to be the spring of living water, in the trenches of discouragement we see Jeremiah question that very same truth as he pours out his discouraged heart to God.

Jeremiah reproaches God and questions if God is instead a spring that fails him. He asks, why is God like a deceitful brook, appearing to have water but turning out to be dry. And why is God silent in the midst of his pain and suffering?

When we get discouraged, it is easy to go down the route of frustration and eventually find ourselves questioning God – why me, why now, why this Lord, why are you not resolving this, why are you silent?

The Response of a gracious God

God answers Jeremiah. We read his response in verses 19-21

*"Therefore, this is what the Lord says; If you **repent**, I will **restore** you, that you may **serve** me; if you utter **worthy**, not worthless words, you will be my spokesman. Let this people turn to you, but you must **not turn to them**. I will make you a wall to this people, a fortified wall of bronze; they will fight against you but will **not overcome you**, for **I am with you** to **rescue** you and **save** you declares the Lord. I will **save you** from the hands of the wicked and redeem you from the grasp of the cruel."* (emphasis mine)

God does not rush in with words of comfort but instead God calls Jeremiah to repent. Why? Is it because Jeremiah questions God, No. God

IN THE DEPTHS OF DISCOURAGEMENT

is not angry with Jeremiah for feeling discouraged, but because he allowed his discouragement to seep into doubting God.

Self-Reflection: When we are discouraged, we have to be cautious to not allow our discouragement to chip away at our core belief in God. The safest place to take our questions is to God, because just as God protected Jeremiah from continuing down that path and correcting him in that moment, he will set us back on the right track too if our questions tend to chip away at our trust in him. God also reassures Jeremiah that he will strengthen, be with him and rescue him but he had to repent first. He had to set his heart, his mind and his words right with God. Jeremiah had to purge those doubtful thoughts of God from his heart and mind. It is always worthwhile to ask God to check our hearts, so that our feelings do not define the truth of who God is, instead God's word and his truth remains the foundation upon which we let our feelings rest.

Faith and doubt cannot co-reside in one's heart. **Matthew 12:34** says *"Out of the overflow of the heart pour out words from your mouth."* What is in our heart will be the utterance of our tongue. It is important to pay attention to what we are focused on during trials. We are indeed allowed to feel a certain way, not brush off our feelings or pretend they do not exist when we come to God. Instead, right beside those emotions, allow the truth of who God is to reside in our hearts, so when doubts assail, they do not shake the foundations of our core beliefs in the Lord. And trust that he will strengthen and restore the faith in us to keep walking in his path. All we can see is our immediate circumstances but God sees the big picture. We might not understand the 'why' of every situation and we do not have to because God comprehends the past, the present and the future.

We see Jeremiah's prayer to God in the mist of his pain. Let's just take a moment and look at Jesus prayer, when he was on the cross, at the height of his pain and persecution. With all that he went through and was going through - He prays *"Father, forgive them, for they do not know what they are doing."* (Luke 23: 34).

💭 *Self-Reflection:* Reading Jesus's words convicts us that all too often we do not respond in a Christ like manner to those that make life difficult for us. How do we pray and show grace to those who make our ministry or our faith walk challenging, do we lose sight of the grace God has extended towards us?

With God's response to Jeremiah in verse 19, *"If you repent, I will restore you, that you may serve me; if you utter worthy, not worthless words, you will be my spokesman. Let this people turn to you, but you must not turn to them.",* we learn four beautiful truths;

- We are reminded of a **promise of restoration when we repent**. Following Jesus is not a call for perfection but an honest relationship with him, which includes taking our doubts and struggles to him and asking him to change our perspective with a repentant heart.
- It reminds us of **our purpose – to serve and glorify him**. We can so often be singularly focused on our circumstances that we tend to forget all that Christ did and continues doing for us – may we look at people and situations through the kingdom lens and extend grace to others.
- We are reminded that **our words are meant to edify, purify, uplift and glorify**. We cannot claim to know God and love him if our words and actions do not testify to that truth.

- We are reminded that **we should not conform to this world,** God is not interested in us becoming more like the world but more like Christ.

Prayer: Lord, when we feel discouraged help us to draw closer to you. Help us fix our gaze on you so that our doubts and a lack of trust in you do not take root. Fill us with your Spirit Lord, so we can faithfully carry on with what you have called us to do. Amen.

Discussion Questions

1. What was Jeremiah asking of God (verse 15). In chapter 14, we read Jeremiah pleading with God for the people and yet here we see differently, what changed?
2. Discuss about responding with grace to those who make life difficult for us?
3. Was Jeremiah out of line in his questioning to God (Verse 18)? Discuss the difference we see in his questioning before (chapter 12:1-4) and over here?
4. In verse 17, what can we glean from how Jeremiah lived among the people of Judah?
5. What was God's response and promise to Jeremiah?
6. Why did Jeremiah have to repent?

In God's response to Jeremiah, we see the promise of restoration, our purpose and that our words matter, discuss about these.

LESSON 8

Where our Hope is Found

My hope is in you, God
Psalm 39:7

 Scripture Passage: ***Jeremiah 16***

Reading through the book of Jeremiah can often draw most of our focus to the inevitable judgement that God was to bring on Judah because of their sinful ways. As this lesson brings us close to the midpoint of our study, let us pause, take a step back and look beyond the standout themes of disobedience and judgement and rest our gaze on the wonderful nature of God. As we take that shift, we find that interspersed within the words from God to his prophet, we get a glimpse into who he is and his heart for his people.

JEREMIAH

1. **A God of grace, forgiveness and reconciliation.**

The repeated warnings to the people of Judah, show us how much God wanted his people to be reconciled to him. He was so patient with his people when repeatedly calling them to repent and turn from their ways. Although he desired for them to be restored to him, he as a holy God could not keep on overlooking their disobedience.

The grace God bestows on us is to never be taken for granted, we are to remember that God is not only a loving, forgiving and merciful Father, but he is also a Holy and Just God. As God's children, some of the consequences we experience is discipline designed to guide us back to God. God disciplines us for our good, in order that we may share in his holiness *(Hebrews 12:10)*.

We are sinful by nature. We don't have to venture far from the beginning of scripture *(Genesis 3)* to know that man has fallen short, sinned and therefore separated from God. Scripture tells us that we will be held accountable for our actions, and our choices do bear an eternal consequence. God in his great mercy made a way for us to be reconciled to him. God took upon himself the ultimate price to make a way for us to be saved – through the blood of Jesus.

In light of the ultimate price Jesus paid for us, how should we live?

Self-Reflection: When we place our faith in him, we automatically are not without sin, as *1 John 4:8* says *"If we claim to be without sin, we deceive ourselves and the truth is not in us."* Our sins are forgiven, yes, but our sinful nature is undergoing a transformation to be more like Christ and that is the work of sanctification that God does in us. And as we journey along, striving to be like him, we will falter and God in his love and mercy will forgive and enable and empower us. But he never forces us, he wants us to willingly come and surrender to him. *Romans 12:1* tells us that we are to offer our bodies as living sacrifices. Living a life that reflects Christ and bringing him glory comes with placing God before our earthly/fleshly desires. And as we desire to do his will and grow in spirit, our intention is for there to be more of God and less of ourselves within us.

2. **God's ways are not necessarily our ways**

Jer 16:1-2 *"Then the word of the Lord came to me "You must not marry and have sons or daughters in this place."*

It might seem harsh for God to forbid Jeremiah from marrying. Why would God give Jeremiah such a command?

The reason for this command is because God is sparing Jeremiah from another decree he had made. *Jeremiah 16:3-4* *"For this is what the Lord says about the sons and daughters born in this land and about the women who are their mothers and the men who are their fathers: They will die of deadly diseases. They will not be mourned or buried but will be like dung lying on the ground. They will perish by sword and famine, and their dead bodies will become food for the birds and the wild animals."*

Self-Reflection: There are times when God withholds things from his people. As in Jeremiah's case, it was not to deny a desire but it was ultimately to spare him from a lot of sorrow in the future. This is a hard aspect of accepting the sovereignty and supremacy of God. At such times, to quell the disappointment in one's heart, it is good to remind ourselves of the truth that God indeed knows what is best. When God says no, it comes from his deep love for us and his all-knowing nature and hence our lack of understanding should be laid with trust at his feet in who he is and his ever-loving nature.

Jeremiah like most others probably had the desire in him to be wed and enjoy the blessings of both marriage and parenthood, yet he was called to make a profound sacrifice in light of the call of God on his life. We often want to live out what *Romans 12:1* calls us to (as living sacrifices) but when it comes time to translate that into reality, often comfort or self wins.

So, how do we like Jeremiah be obedient to God's will for us that might be far removed from our heart's desire?

It begins with a purposeful pursuit of God, not neglecting his word and time spent sitting at his feet. This forms the crux of our pursuit of him, which then pours into all areas of our life. God renews us from within, the work that he does in us is a change that begins from within and is reflected in the fruit that can be seen by all.

In verses 5 and 8 we also read of God telling Jeremiah to refrain from joining the people in mourning or feasting. For Jeremiah, it would have very much felt similar to a self-imposed exile from his community, further adding to his lonely walk and also in some ways making it more difficult to get them to listen to his words while being so removed from them. And it probably could have also contributed to further angering some of the people against him.

Self-Reflection: Jeremiah had to let go and surrender to God's command. He kept God's will above his desires and comfort. God commanded Jeremiah to let go of a desire to spare him of future pain and heartache. Is God asking you to let go of a desire? In walking the righteous path, maybe we have to let go of something that God is asking us to, it may be difficult, but may we in obedience surrender our desires to God, and trust that all that he says is for our good.

3. **A God who is not obscure with what he expects of the people.**

In *Jeremiah 16:10-11*, God says, when the people ask you (Jeremiah) why God has decreed such a disaster on us, what wrong have we done, tell them, it was because they forsook me, followed, served and worshipped other gods. We see God repeatedly point out the specific reason behind his decision. God does not leave the people guessing. What they endure, is caused by their repeated prolonged disobedience which led to God's favour no longer being upon them *(Jeremiah 16:13)*. And the reason for the clarity is so that the people would understand and repent.

With clarity we know the way to be restored to God, Jesus said in *John 14:6 "I am the way, the truth and the life, no one comes to the Father except through me."*

Scripture with clarity also teaches us that we cannot serve two masters *(Matthew 6:24)*. The Israelites went after other gods.

Self-Reflection: What are we in pursuit of? What are we bending the knee to when it comes to our worship? We worship that which we regard and believe in - is that wealth, work, your assets, your image. What in your life comes before God?

Psalm 119:2 says *"Blessed are those who keep his statutes and seek him with all their heart"*

When we are truly seeking him with all our heart, our hearts are aligned to him and so are our desires. Genuinely seeking God, causes our desires, delight and pursuit to be nothing else but God and everything else finds its right position and perspective.

4. **A God who pursues**

In ***Jeremiah 16:11-12,*** God says, *"your fathers forsook me, but you have behaved more wickedly than your fathers. See how each of you is following the stubbornness of his evil heart instead of obeying me."*

God had been speaking to the Israelites since their fathers turned away from him. His pursuit of them was not a few days or a few months old, he had been pursuing them for generations. We get to see a God who does not give up on those that he calls his.

Self-Reflection: God does not give up on you or me because we have been struggling with sin in our lives. If we look at Peter, at his moment of fear and weakness, he denied Jesus. Did Jesus give up on him – no, he did not and he is the same with us.

When we are not walking right with God, we can harbour the notion that God's ardour for us cools down a bit, but in truth it does not. We move away from him when we sin, so we do not feel his intimacy as we should. In the story of the prodigal son *(Luke 15:11-32),* the son was not sure how the father would respond when he would return to him. The son was distant and disconnected from the father and therefore could not sense and feel the fathers love for him. It is the same with us, we do not sense our Heavenly Father's love for us when we have moved away from him. How does the prodigal son's father respond? He does not just put up with the son upon his return, he runs to him, embraces him and restores him to his rightful place as his child. What a picture of grace, forgiveness and love. That is who God is – let not guilt or shame keep you from turning to God. He is calling you.

5. A Faithful God

Even though his people repeatedly falter in following him, God continued to be faithful to them. As a holy and just God, he does not overlook intentional repeated sin, but interspersed with the consequence of sin is the promise of their restoration *(Jeremiah 16:15)*.

Self-Reflection: The people of Israel had other things that drew their focus and worship from God. Similarly, there are many distractions for us that tempt us to turn our back to God. We might not necessarily entirely turn from him, but there might be aspects of our life that we have kept turned away from God, that we have kept from entirely surrendering to him. And even when his voice calls us or convicts us to surrender those areas to him, we remain stubborn and turned away. By doing so, we are keeping his light from shining in those areas. Turn to him, face him entirely, let his light shine on every area of your life and through you to others. Let us leave no room for the enemy's darkness to harbour, let us give it all to God. He is a faithful God, who never leaves you or forsakes you.

God is where our hope is found. His voice is calling you to accept him, to submit and to lay your burdens on him. Follow him with delight, purpose, obedience and a servant heart.

Prayer: Lord, thank you for being a loving and faithful Father. There are times when we struggle to understand what you ask of us, in those moments help us to trust in who you are. Lord, help us to stay rooted in your word and grow in our understanding of you. There is no greater gift than to be reconciled to you. Thank you, Lord for never giving up on us and that we always have hope in you. Amen.

Discussion Questions

1. What three things did God tell Jeremiah not to do? (16:2, 5, 8)? What does this reveal to us about God?
2. What significance was this meant to reflect on Jeremiah's preaching and what impact this might have had on Jeremiah personally?
3. When God says no to something that we very much desire, how do we reconcile and accept God's 'no'?
4. We all have heard the saying 'God hates the sin but loves the sinner.' Talk about practically living this out? Think about any personal life examples and share if it is fine to do so.
5. The people of Judah even though they knew with clarity what God wanted of them, refused to accept it. What truths in scripture although clearly stated, can be a struggle for you to accept and live out?
6. Discuss if and how God's judgement and restoration can serve to magnify the name and power of God?

LESSON 9

Commit your cause to God

*"May the Lord be praised, day after day he bears
our burdens, God is our salvation."*
Psalm 68:19

 Scripture Passage: ***Jeremiah 20***

In Jeremiah ch 20, we see opposition to prophet Jeremiah beginning to intensify. The start of the chapter gives us a glimpse into his persecution at the hands of those who did not want to heed God's word. Pashhur, the chief officer in the temple, heard Jeremiah prophesying and had him beaten and put in the stocks (verse 2). Jeremiah was subject to painful public disgrace and was regarded as a false prophet.

It was ironic that Pashhur being a priest, was not willing to listen to words of warning from God. Also notable is that all the torture and humiliation inflicted on Jeremiah at the behest of Pashhur, was done in the house of the Lord (verse 2, at the upper Gate of Benjamin at the Lord's temple). The temple was the place where the priest held power and Pashhur used it to defy the authority of God. He clearly was no man of God for he did not fear what God had to say or his authority, neither had he the discernment to know what was from God. He guided people away from God and humiliated and inflicted pain on those who were obedient to God, like Jeremiah.

Self-Reflection: A position of leadership or influence within the church does not automatically imply that the person is living a life that is right with God and neither do their words or perspective always equate to the truth. Each and every one of us are to read the word and discern and see if those who occupy those places are in submission to God *(Dear friends, do not believe every spirit, but test the spirits to see whether they are from God, because many false prophets have gone out into the world, 1 John 4:1).*

We can err in our ways by leaning towards taking someone else's interpretation of scripture without studying the word of God for ourselves. The Lord blesses us with great biblical teachers who help us understand the word, but may we remember that they are after all human and we have to be cautious to not impetuously believe one person's teachings or interpretation over the word of God, because if we do that, we leave ourselves open to being led astray in our understanding of scripture and regarding their words and thoughts above God's.

Invited to share our heart with God

Jeremiah with his heart heavy, pours out his burden to the Lord. He complains and attributes his suffering to the Lord. In *Jeremiah 1,* we saw that Jeremiah was reluctant to be a prophet, but God says that he chose him to be one. And in this chapter, Jeremiah says that all he gets as a prophet is insult and reproach.

Jeremiah shares that he was torn between the tension within himself of not wanting to proclaim God's word because of what it subjects him to, and yet he could not keep from his calling of speaking out God's word. Prophetic reluctance over divine compulsion is what we see here described.

Self-Reflection: We are invited to share our heart as is with the Lord, Jeremiah did not soften his words or his emotions when he spoke to God. He was completely honest with what he felt. This is such an encouraging reminder for us to know that we do not have to polish our heavy emotions before we take them to the Lord, or even our hesitation or struggle with being obedient to his calling. God wants us to approach him in humility and honesty with our struggles because he will minister to our needs accordingly. We also saw Jeremiah pour out his genuine emotions to God in previous lessons (lesson 4 and 7), a reminder that it is okay to go to God repeatedly if we are struggling with something specific and allow him to comfort and strengthen us each of those times. God invites us to go to him with our burdens as *Psalm 68:19* so beautifully reminds us *"May the Lord be praised, day after day he bears our burdens, God is our salvation."*

Faith strengthened

In verse 11-13, we see Jeremiah's faith strengthen. The first thing he reminds himself of and is comforted by is the continual presence of God with him like a mighty warrior. Through it all, there was no doubt about God being with him. God's presence strengthened and sustained him, and he reminded himself that nothing can stand against God, his plans and his purposes.

Self-Reflection: May we remember that the Lord is with us through any situation we might be going through. He will never leave us or forsake us. Draw strength from this truth and know that no scheme of Satan will prevail against the plans of God. Stand firm in his strength and rest in the truth of his faithful presence.

Commune with God

Deep in despair, heart heavy, very much in the midst of his trying circumstance, Jeremiah found himself being strengthened as he communed with God.

Self-Reflection: This is a wonderful reminder for us that there is so much power in prayer. Often times when things worry us, we can spend many a minute fretting over it, and fail to take it to God as often as we should, allowing those worrying thoughts to fill our minds. I am guilty of doing that, I have to remind myself that instead of thinking and worrying about it so much let me take it to God in prayer and that has been such a game changer for me. It is something that I have to constantly be intentional about.

Jeremiah portrays that the impossibility of enduring and going through his situation is made a possibility because of God and he says in verse 12b *"For to you I have committed my cause."*

I found these words very encouraging and my prayer is that they serve as an encouragement to you too.

What cause lays heavy on your heart today?

Is it your health or that of a loved one, your financial situation, lack of work, a strained relationship, the mental health of a dear one, the spiritual state of a spouse, a child, sibling or friend? Whatever it is, know that just as Jeremiah did not have to see through his cause on his own strength, but instead committed it to God, so can we.

So, dear friends commit that which causes your heart to be heavy and your mind to worry to God. Commit it to him because he is your mighty warrior, your ever-present help, your rock and your fortress, your provider and protector, your Sovereign God and your loving heavenly Father who created you, sees you, hears you and cares for you.

Prayer: Lord, we thank you that you hear our each and every cry. Thank you that we can come to you again and again with what assails us and pour out what lies in our hearts and know that you will carry our burden. Help us to hold onto the truth that you are faithful and always with us and that we do not have to carry the cause that which lays heavy on our hearts on our own. Amen.

Discussion Questions

1. At the start of the chapter (Ch 20), where do we find Jeremiah?
2. Who was Passhur? What cautionary lesson can we take away from how he regarded the word of God and his prophet?
3. What does Jeremiah do in 20:7-13? Does this reaction surprise you? Why or why not?
4. Jeremiah says 'You deceived me Lord and I was deceived' what do you think Jeremiah was referring to here, Was this true? How might we fall into the same line of thinking as Jeremiah?
5. What do we see happening to Jeremiah's faith as he shares his heart with God (20:11-13)?

To what does Jeremiah return to in 20:14-18? Discuss this especially considering the context of his words in 20:11-13? What can we learn from this?

LESSON 10

Two Baskets of Figs

The eyes of the lord are on the righteous and his ears attentive to their cry
Psalm 34:15

 Scripture Passage: ***Jeremiah 24***

Jeremiah 24: 2 *"One basket had very good figs, like those that ripen early; the other basket, very poor figs, so bad that they could not be eaten."*

This image was given by God to Jeremiah. It was when the first exiles were carried from Jerusalem to Babylon by king Nebuchadnezzar.

The Lord showed Jeremiah the two baskets of figs placed in front of the temple of the Lord. The front of the temple was the place where the people brought their offerings. With where the baskets were placed, the two baskets of figs seem to represent two kinds of offerings to the Lord.

Offerings were a form of worship or devotion to God. Both the baskets contained figs, the only disparity was in the quality of the figs. But, when brought as an offering to God, the contrast in the quality of the contents of the basket makes all the difference as it reflects one's attitude towards God.

💭 *Self-Reflection:* We can offer different things to God, our time, talents or finances. But the act of bringing forth an offering alone is not what God is after because he sees the heart and the devotion behind it. What we offer to God is meant to serve others and bring him glory and not point to self for praise.

God goes on to explain to Jeremiah that the good figs represent those that have been taken captive to Babylon, and the bad figs are the ones who remain in Jerusalem.

The good figs were those who were faithful to God, they were the ones God was going to restore to the land.

Being taken first as exiles by the enemies seems really awful, how then can they be the good figs. Contrary to what we would automatically assume of being taken first as captives, they were the ones who were removed first by God and thereby did not remain in Jerusalem while it endured God's judgement.

💭 *Self-Reflection:* When we find ourselves in a bad place and things just seem to be going from bad to worse, similar to those first exiles, although we do not see it yet, let us trust the almighty God who is very much working in those situations to lift us out of that valley and set our feet upon a rock again. With hope and trust, may we stay faithful to him through it all and hold fast to what *Romans 8:28 says "And we know that in all things God works for the good of all those who love him and are called according to his purpose."*

David Guzik says "Judgement upon a nation or community means that all endure some suffering, even those who are faithful to God through it. But God knows the difference between those who were caught up in the judgement and those who brought down the judgement."

God's thoughts and ways are indeed not our thoughts and ways. Even when the first exiles probably entertained notions that God had turned away from them, he was working for them, ensuring that they did not experience his catastrophic judgement on Jerusalem. And God not only protected them then, but was right there planning not only to restore them in his time but also that he would bless them during the time of their exile.

In **Jeremiah 24: 6-7** we read *"My eyes will **watch over them** for their good, and I will bring them back to this land. I will **build them up** and not tear them down; I will **plant them** and not uproot them. I will **give them a heart to know me**, that I am the Lord. They will **be my people,** and **I will be their God,** for they will return to me with all their heart."(emphasis mine)*

We see a promise of **physical restoration** when God says that he will build them up and plant them. But we also see a promise of **spiritual restoration**, when God says that he will give them the desire to know him and that they would return to him and follow him with all of their heart. Their devotion to God would not be fragmented but wholehearted.

We read on in Jeremiah 29, that God did not plan for them to just wait on their time for restoration but they were to live their lives to the full while they waited. Their time in captivity would not be easy but the Lord's hand on them would make it possible to overcome those challenges.

Jeremiah 29:4-7 *"This is what the Lord Almighty, the God of Israel, says to all those I carried into exile from Jerusalem to Babylon: "**Build houses and settle down; plant gardens** and eat what they produce. **Marry** and have sons and daughters; find wives for your sons and give your daughters in marriage, so that they too may have sons and daughters. Increase in number there; do not decrease. Also, seek the peace and prosperity of the city to which I have carried you into exile. Pray to the Lord for it, because if it prospers, you too will prosper." (emphasis mine)*

Self-Reflection: This is a picture of promise, hope and restoration. A reminder that in the worst of situations, he still is our God, he has a plan for us, he never forsakes us, he is working for us in the midst of those valley moments and most importantly he is not just our God when things are going well but he is very much our Sovereign Lord in ALL situations.

If anyone is in a period of waiting on God, like the people in captivity waiting upon God to restore them, we wait with an anticipation and expectation and continue to live our lives that way. He does not expect our life to be on a standstill but we keep on living, faithfully to him, because we trust in his ways, his plans and his purposes for us.

In Jeremiah 29: 11 God says about the exiles *"For I know the plans I have for you," declares the Lord, "plans to prosper you and not to harm you, plans to give you hope and a future."*

As we looked at this passage of scripture from Jeremiah, we are reminded to reflect on what kind of offering we are to God, would we be good figs or bad ones. Do we hold onto God through every distraction thrown at us and through all challenging situations? Those good figs were the ones who were surrounded by many who stubbornly followed their own evil hearts and rebelled against God (bad figs). Feels like a very parallel representation of times today, but in the midst of it all, they remained faithful and as God says *"As the good figs, I regard them as good (Jeremiah 24:5)."*

Prayer: Lord, hep us to choose you every day, through the good and the difficult times. May we always honour you with our obedience and our worship. May we continue to be faithful to you and perseverant through all of our days. Amen.

TWO BASKETS OF FIGS

 Discussion Questions

1. When was Jeremiah shown the two baskets of figs?
2. Where were the two baskets placed and what does that signify?
3. What kind of offerings do we place in front of the Lord? What does this passage remind us of to be aware of with regards to our offerings?
4. What do the good and bad figs represent?
5. What do you think the group of exiles would have felt and concluded about the situation they found themselves in? What can we learn from this situation?
6. What did God promise to do in their lives when they were in Babylon? What encouragement can we take from this?

What about God do we learn through this passage and what is God speaking to you through it?

LESSON 11

Truth or Falsehood

"Be on your guard against false prophets; they come to you in sheep's clothing, but inwardly they are ferocious wolves.
Matthew 7:15

 Scripture Passage: *Jeremiah 28*

Jeremiah is confronted by a false prophet Hananiah. Hananiah stands in the temple of the Lord before the priests and all the people and prophesises a very different future to what Jeremiah had been speaking about all along.

In *Jeremiah 28: 2-3*, Hananiah says, *"This is what the Lord Almighty, the God of Israel, says: 'I will break the yoke of the king of Babylon.* **Within two years** *I will bring back to this place all the articles of the Lord's house that Nebuchadnezzar king of Babylon removed from here and took to Babylon."* (emphasis mine)

Observations on how and what Hananiah spoke:

> Hananiah begins with a time period – the yoke of Babylon will be broken in **two years** which is in sharp contrast to what Jeremiah had said in ch 25v11 *"This whole country will become a desolate wasteland, and these nations will serve the king of Babylon **seventy years**."* (emphasis mine).

The drastic reduction in the duration of their difficulty would have surely perked up ears and compelled people to reason with the want to believe Hananiah.

Self-Reflection: At times, we do not want to come to terms with what God might be asking us to walk through, so we cling to what may sound better or less difficult rather than the truth from God.

> Hananiah claimed to speak in the name of the Lord, the wording being exactly what Jeremiah would say; *"This is what the Lord Almighty, the God of Israel, says"*

Although Hananiah begins his prophecy in a manner similar to how Jeremiah would speak, his words were not from God. When we read Hananiah's words it is easy for us to see them as false because we read them through the lens of prior knowledge that Hananiah was a false prophet.

Self-Reflection: When we listen to teaching/preaching now, we should not presume that the words spoken are always in alignment with scripture. We have to always remain cautious. There is a saying that *false teaching is more often **not** between right and wrong teaching, but rather between right and almost right teaching.* And that small shift in the truth is often what can dull the natural tendency to be wary of what someone says as most of it would sound accurate. When something sounds almost right, there is a greater chance for that false theology/teaching to be believed unless one is well versed with scripture or takes the time to test and see if what was said is in accordance with scripture.

> Hananiah spoke with boldness and confidence, which probably worked in his favour, convincing people that he was actually speaking a true prophecy. He confidently proclaimed these words in the temple of the Lord, in the presence of Jeremiah, the priests and all the people and claimed them to be from God.

That perceived boldness did not stem from the knowledge that he was doing the work of God, but rather from a lack of fear of the Lord. For if Hananiah truly did believe what he said (that the Lord is almighty and is the God of Israel), he would not dare to speak out of his own accord and claim it to be from God.

Self-Reflection: Often inaccurate teachings cloaked with boldness and confidence can be perceived subconsciously with a notion of correctness. The tone of the voice, the stance on the pulpit or the sheer number of people listening can be a snare, but it does not make one a truthful mouthpiece of God.

> What Hananiah did not speak within this prophecy also reveals a lot to the truth of its origin.

When we read through the earlier chapters of Jeremiah, there is no missing the clarity with which God mentions the reason why he intended to bring doom upon the nation. They were rebellious, had turned away from him and were worshipping other gods *(Jeremiah 2:13)*. And God sends word through Jeremiah repeatedly about the need for repentance that is sincere and nor perfunctory *(Jeremiah 4:1-2)*.

Hananiah prophesises a quick restoration to peace but there is no acknowledgement of the sins of the people and the need for genuine repentance and a change of their ways. Hananiah's words catered to what the people probably found more appealing and easier to accept.

Self-Reflection: Often when God convicts us to change a sinful habit or our wrong approach to something, it is not always easy. Our tendency can lean towards seeking help from God with minimal to no effort on self-reflection and change from our end. But as a speaker once said, "God seeks our conformation more than our comfort."

As God works in us to build us up and sanctify us, he would never make compromises on our spiritual state, it is us who tend to look for compromises. We might not enjoy the pruning and refining process of God, but all that he brings about will always be good for us because he is a God who is perfect, good and holy.

How did Jeremiah respond to Hananiah:

Jeremiah was not motivated to dispel Hananiah's wrong prophecy by

- His pride – as Hananiah makes him appear as a liar.
- By his anger – how dare Hananiah challenge his words which were indeed from God.
- By fear – of the consequences of what the people might do to him if they believed him to be prophesying incorrectly and always of doom.

Jeremiah responds by reminding people of previous prophecies and says that if what Hananiah said is truly from God, it will come to pass *(Jeremiah 28:8-9)*.

Self-Reflection: When our faith or differing theological views are challenged, let not our responses be driven by our own emotions or desire to be proved right. We do not reflect Christ when we do that. With kindness, compassion and respect, point to the word and encourage to pore over scripture along with prayer for wisdom and discernment as 1 john 4:1 says *"Dear friends, do not believe everyone who claims to speak by the Spirit. You must test them to see if the spirit they have comes from God. For there are many false prophets in the world."*

Prayer: Lord, thank you for your word that we can rely on, for the promise of wisdom and discernment to know what is from you and what is not. May we study your word and know that if we turn to you, you will shield us from taking steps that lead away from you. Amen.

TRUTH OR FALSEHOOD

 Discussion Questions

1. Who contradicts Jeremiah. What specifically did he prophesy?
2. Break down all the different things that Hananiah prophesises in contradiction to Jeremiah and what applications can we take away?
3. Discuss other ways that are helpful in recognising and guarding against false teachers?
4. Share any of your favourite verses in scripture that warn and instruct us about false teachers?
5. How did Hananiah illustrate his prophecy in 28:10-11? How did Jeremiah respond?
6. What was God's response to Hananiah in 28:12-17? What would be his punishment?

What does this passage teach us about how best to respond when we encounter someone who challenges our faith or theology?

LESSON 12

A Heart of Obedience

Is God's word and his Authority Shaping your Life

 Scripture Passage: ***Jeremiah 35***

In Jeremiah 35, we read about a group of people called the Recabites, whom God uses as an example of obedience and a rebuke to the people of Judah.

Who are the Recabites?

They were a nomadic group of people related to the Kenites *(1 Chronicles 2:55)*, some of whom lived among and near the Israelites. Moses' father-in-law, Jethro, also known as Reuel, was 'the priest of Midian' and a Kenite *(Judges 1:16)*. Moses lived among the Kenites for many years before God called him as the one to deliver the Israelites from their enslavement in Egypt. Some Kenites, including Jethro moved along with Moses and the people of God.

(https://www.gotquestions.org/Kenites.html).

Jeremiah 35 details the command their forefather Jonadab gave them to follow.

What was the command?

They were not to drink wine, never to build houses, sow seed or plant vineyards; never have any of these things, but must always live in tents. And the resulting blessing was that they would live a long time in the land as nomads *(Jer 35:6-7)*.

This command was given by Jonadab (also spelled as Jehonadab), the son of Rekab. This was the Jehonadab who we read about in *2 Kings 10*, who helped King Jehu destroy Baal worship temporarily at the time. This would be over 200 years prior to Jeremiah's time.

God tells Jeremiah to go to the Recabite family, bring them to the temple of the Lord and offer them some wine to drink. Jeremiah follows the Lord's instruction, but the Recabites do not touch the wine and explain the reason behind it. They say *"We have obeyed everything our forefather Jehonadab son of Rekab commanded us." (Jeremiah 35:8)*

Taking note of the time Jehonadab lived, it makes the command he gave to his descendants over 200 years old. God says to Jeremiah in verse 14 *'Jehonadab son of Rekab ordered his descendants not to drink wine and this command has been kept. To this day they do not drink wine, because they obey their forefather's command. But I have spoken to you again and again, yet you have not obeyed me."*

When we read the command the Recabites lived by, we can tend to focus on the type of command and the blessing connected to it. When we focus on the practices, we miss the principle behind it. When God points to the Recabites as an example, he does not intend for his people to follow the Recabite ways. God points to the principle behind their ways, their obedience.

The Recabites, did not try to fit in and mould themselves to how others around them lived. They stayed true and loyal to what they were commanded to do. Their lifestyle/choices stayed true to what they believed in and it was not up for compromise. When they were offered wine, they did not imbibe a little just to appease anyone, they did not bend their rules for acceptance, benefit or anything else. They most definitely would not have been perfect in how they led their lives (as all men are sinners and fall short of the glory of God), but their heart of obedience was noteworthy for God to mention it.

Obedience matters to God.

Their obedience contrasts Judah's disobedience towards God. The Recabite's lives were shaped around the word and authority of their forefather Jehonadab.

Self-Reflection: Is God's word the ultimate authority in your life? And if so, how is your life being shaped by the word and authority of God?

What is Obedience in a biblical sense?

According to *Holman's Illustrated Bible Dictionary*, a definition of biblical obedience is "to hear God's Word and act accordingly."

Eerdman's Bible Dictionary states, "True 'hearing,' or obedience, involves the physical hearing that inspires the hearer, and a belief or trust that in turn motivates the hearer to act in accordance with the speaker's desires."

Self-Reflection: Obedience comes not out of compulsion but from faith.

God calls us to a life of obedience to Him

Romans 1:5 says "Through him we received grace and apostleship to call all the Gentiles to the obedience that comes from faith for his name's sake."

1 Peter 1:1-2 says "To God's elect chosen to be obedient to Jesus Christ and sprinkled with his blood."

Self-Reflection: Obedience to God and a life lived as a follower of Jesus go hand in hand. Our obedience comes from our faith, as a natural outpouring from the desire within to submit to him and do his will.

God delights in our obedience.

1 Samuel 15:22 "What is more pleasing to the LORD: your burnt offerings and sacrifices or your obedience to his voice? Listen! Obedience is better than sacrifice, and submission is better than offering the fat of rams."

Psalm 128:1 says "Blessed are all who fear the Lord, who walk in obedience to him."

Self-Reflection: God delights in wholehearted devotion to him. Nothing pleases him more than willing worship and devotion that stem from the desire to walk in obedience to him not for what he can do for us but just because of who he is.

Obedience reflects our hearts posture

John 14:23 says "Anyone who loves me will obey my teaching."
2 John 6 says "And this is love that we walk in obedience to His commands."
John 15:14 "You are my friends if you do what I command."

💭 *Self-Reflection:* Our willingness to obey often serves to check where our hearts lie. Our desires may not always align with that of God, but as we grow in spirit and faith, God realigns our desires that reflect more of him in us. When we struggle to obey, may we turn to God and seek his help.

Obedience leads to Righteousness

Romans 6:16 says "Don't you know that when you offer yourselves to someone as obedient slaves, you are slaves of the one you obey—whether you are slaves to sin, which leads to death, or to obedience, which leads to righteousness"

💭 *Self-Reflection:* God's word calls us to live a life of obedience to him. Each of us need the grace of God to be able to live a life surrendered to him. Under his grace we obey neither to gain his approval, nor because he commanded it but because God desires it. We are to set our mind on things above *(Colossians 3:2),* and living a life of obedience aligns our heart with God.

An obedient heart is a worshipful heart, it is an outpouring of our faith and trust in him, of his presence and the evidence of his Lordship in our life.

As *James 1:22* says, may we not just be listeners of the word but do what it says.

Prayer: Lord, may our hearts and our desires be aligned with you. May we delight in doing your will, honouring you with our obedience and finding joy in the things of the Lord. Grow us in obedience and in discipleship to you. Amen.

A HEART OF OBEDIENCE

 Discussion Questions

1. Who were the Recabites?
2. What did God instruct Jeremiah to do? How do you think the Recabites would have viewed this whole process?
3. How does this make us view some of the tests we go through?
4. What was the command, and the reason the Recabites gave for following their forefather Jonadab's command?
5. What point was God making through the Recabites?
6. Why is Obedience to God important to Him?

When following God is not easy, how can we encourage ourselves to stay obedient?

LESSON 13

Consistent Communion with God

Communion is a glorious fellowship with God, that our union with Him makes a joyful possibility

 Scripture Passage – **Jeremiah Chapters 36-39**

'Then the word of the Lord came to Jeremiah' - we read this sentence time and time again throughout the book of Jeremiah. He was a prophet chosen by God, and hence we are not taken by surprise when we come across those words. But Jeremiah was after all a man, who although chosen, equipped and strengthened by God to be his prophet *(Jeremiah 1:9-10, 17-19)*, experienced human struggles, fears and emotions. He was challenged to be strong and stay obedient to God's call on his life despite the fear within when the people got hostile. He struggled to not despair, and leaned towards giving up when the people refused to repent and continued to carry on in their idolatry. Like all of us, he did have his moments where he wanted to give up doing what God was asking of Him *(Jeremiah 15)*.

Jeremiah was guided by God to proclaim that the nation of Judah would suffer famine, foreign conquest, plunder, and captivity in a land of strangers. His message of doom did not sit well with his hearers and as a consequence he underwent quite a lot of difficulties at their hands.

Jeremiah chapters 36 to 39 details some of the persecution Jeremiah faced. While we read through these four chapters, we can easily see Jeremiah's suffering as a running thread through them. But in the midst of his toughest times, let us not miss the consistency and continuity with which Jeremiah communed with God.

There are at least six instances in these four chapters where we read that the word of the Lord came to Jeremiah.

Jeremiah 36:1 "In the fourth year of Jehoiakim son of Josiah king of Judah, this word came to Jeremiah from the Lord"

Jeremiah 36:27 "After the king burned the scroll containing the words that Baruch had written at Jeremiah's dictation, the word of the Lord came to Jeremiah"

Jeremiah 37:6-7a "Then the word of the Lord came to Jeremiah the prophet"

The above mentioned three times that Jeremiah received a word from God was just prior to him being arrested and put in prison. Just before he was put in prison, he was in hiding from King Jehoiakim so as to evade being arrested *(Jeremiah 36)*.

In the next section of scripture, *Jeremiah 37*, we get to know that he was falsely accused, arrested, beaten and put in the dungeon where he remained a long time. And in the dungeon, he continues communing with God and he receives a word from God for king Zedekiah *(Jeremiah 37:11-14)*

Jeremiah 37: 16-17 "Jeremiah was put into a vaulted cell in a dungeon, where he remained a long time. Then King Zedekiah sent for him and had him brought to the palace, where he asked him privately, "Is there any word from the Lord?" "Yes," Jeremiah replied, "you will be delivered into the hands of the king of Babylon."

In *Jeremiah 38:6* we read that Jeremiah was put into a cistern *"So they took Jeremiah and put him into the cistern of Malkijah, the king's son, which was in the courtyard of the guard. They lowered Jeremiah by ropes into the cistern; it had no water in it, only mud, and Jeremiah sank down into the mud."*

He was later taken out of the cistern and placed in the courtyard of the guard, it was not as harsh a place as the dungeon and the cistern, but he was still a prisoner.

While Jeremiah was a prisoner in the courtyard of the guard, King Zedekiah seeks Jeremiah out to know if there is a word from God. Jeremiah had a request before he would say anything. He says *"Jeremiah said to Zedekiah, if I give you an answer, will you not kill me? Even if I did give you counsel will you not listen to me." (Jeremiah 38:15)*. To which king Zedekiah swears an oath that he would not kill Jeremiah or hand him over to those that seek to do so *(Jeremiah 38:16)* and then Jeremiah shared God's word with Zedekiah *(Jeremiah 38:17)*.

We read on in *Jeremiah 39:15 "While Jeremiah had been confined in the courtyard of the guard, the word of the Lord came to him"*

We get a clear picture that Jeremiah lived with a constant possibility of his life being taken. With such a possibility looming over him, he did not turn away from God or allow his circumstances to become a barrier in his time with God. From these four chapters, we saw Jeremiah receive a word from God six times, the first three before he was beaten, arrested and prisoned. And the next three times was when he was prisoned in various places. Jeremiah does not seem to grumble at God for ensuring that he did not spare Jeremiah from enduring persecution, but even through it he seemed to surrender and commune with the Almighty.

Self-Reflection: Be it the depths and darkness of the dungeon, the pit of the cistern or the guard's prison, Jeremiah continued communing with God, receives God's word and continues to be his servant, fulfilling his role and purpose as God's prophet no matter the situation he found himself in. His communing with God was not dependent on his circumstances, his emotions or fears but instead continued despite them. What a lesson for us all.

The enemy knows the power that comes from our consistently drawing near to God through prayer and time with him, and he will try his hardest to make us stumble in this aspect. So how do we press through? It begins with a choice that we have to make even when we do not feel like talking to God. In those moments we do not rely on our feelings, but on the truth that God will hear us and is near us when we call on him. The truth that he is the source of our strength and comfort and through him we can overcome. And as we intentionally make that choice to draw near to him our faith is bolstered and as we press through, our continual communing with God will help sustain us through our toughest moments and we can speak scripture to ourselves to strengthen our soul.

Verses we can hold onto when we feel weak and helpless,

Exodus 15:2 "The Lord is my strength and my defence; he has become my salvation. He is my God, and I will praise him, my father's God, and I will exalt him.

Habakkuk 3:19 "The Sovereign Lord is my strength; he makes my feet like the feet of a deer, he enables me to tread on the heights."

Psalm 59:17 "You are my strength, I sing praise to you; you, God, are my fortress, my God on whom I can rely."

Self-Reflection: Through our challenges, may we take our emotions and our struggles to God, keeping our focus on God rather than the situation, so that we remain tethered to his word, his promises and the hope we have in him. Our God is steadfast and faithful.

Is our devotion, worship and our hearts posture towards him consistent through our own personal pits and prisons? Do we in all circumstances, pursue him, stay focused on him and quiet our hearts and minds to hear from him. Through each and every situation Jeremiah faced, God continued to use him as a prophet. We are reminded that God can use every situation in our lives for our good and for his plans and purposes.

Prayer: Lord, forgive us when we so easily get our circumstances to overcome our thoughts and emotions and let slip our communion with you. May we always remember the words of *Psalm 121:1-2, "I lift up my eyes to the hills, where does my help come from. My help comes from the Lord the maker of heaven and earth."* Through every valley, help us to fix our gaze on you, pursue you, seek to hear from you and help us to remain obedient, grow spiritually and be used by you for your kingdom purposes. Amen.

Discussion Questions

1. Through ch 36-39, we see a running thread of persecution Jeremiah faced. What else do we see the prophet consistently do during that time?
2. What are some of the common barriers to communication with God?

How did Jeremiah press through? What can we glean from it to help our communication and worship of God when we find ourselves in difficult seasons?

LESSON 14

Trustworthy Father

The Lord is trustworthy in all he promises and faithful in all he does
Psalm 145:13

 Scripture Passage: **Jeremiah 39:5-18 and 40:1-6**

What was happening in Jerusalem at this time?

Jerusalem had fallen captive to the Babylonians led by King Nebuchadnezzar, and chapter 40 begins with the aftermath of the fall.

What was happening with Jeremiah?

Jeremiah found himself bound in chains among the captives from Jerusalem and Judah who were being carried into exile to Babylon *(Jeremiah 40:1)*.

In chapter, 39 verses 11-12 we *read "Now Nebuchadnezzar king of Babylon had given these orders about Jeremiah through Nebuzaradan, commander of the imperial guard, take him and look after him, don't harm him but do for him whatever he asks."*

Despite Nebuchadnezzar's command for considerate treatment towards Jeremiah, at this point (chained and among the exiles) Jeremiah would have probably resigned himself to a fate of being an exile in Babylon.

As a prophet, he was not treated too kindly by his own people, so it would not be unexpected to presume that Jeremiah was not anticipating the Babylonians to treat him with much respect or to keep their word (Nebuchadnezzar's order).

While in chains, bound and headed to Babylon, comes an unexpected turn of events. Nebuzaradan, the commander of King Nebuchadnezzar's guard recognises Jeremiah among the exiles and frees him.

The commander says in verses 2-4 *"When the commander of the guard found Jeremiah, he said to him, "The Lord your God decreed this disaster for this place. And now the Lord has brought it about; he has done just as he said he would. All this happened because you people sinned against the Lord and did not obey him. But today I am freeing you from the chains on your wrists."*

Self-Reflection: God works in unexpected ways and many a times when we least expect it. God made a way for Jeremiah; Scripture reminds us time and time again to not fear because God is with us. Knowing this truth passively is one thing but actively living it out in the midst of turmoil is something that we cannot do in our own strength.

Reflecting on all that Jeremiah went through while staying obedient to God, and after the fall of Jerusalem, finding himself chained to be taken forcibly among the exiles, he could easily have felt frustrated and angry at God. We know that it can be easy to start reacting in the flesh when things start falling apart. But Jeremiah stood firm on God's word to him *"Do not be afraid for I am with you." (Jeremiah 1:8). "For I am with you and will rescue you." (Jeremiah 1:19b)*

JEREMIAH

Self-Reflection: At times in our lives, we look for a door to open, to get out of a miserable situation, for a new opportunity or a lifeline thrown from God. But as my mum once said to me, our job is to keep walking along in the corridor of life surrendering to God and only when we approach and are close enough to those sliding doors, will they open, not when we are at the start of the corridor or any place in between. God's timing can often be like that, the doors will seem shut, it may seem pointless to keep walking faithfully when we don't see any plausible way out or through, but just as we know those sliding doors will open only when we get right in front of it, we got to trust and walk on in the path that God is leading and guiding us on and trust that when the time is right, he will make a way.

God is our Jehovah Jireh; he provides for us, maybe not in the way we expect but the promise is that he will.

Philippians 4:19. "*And my God will supply all your needs according to His riches in glory in Christ Jesus.*"

Let's take a look at the provision God gives Jeremiah through the Babylonian in this chapter.

Jeremiah 40: 4-6 "*But today I am freeing you from the chains on your wrists. Come with me to Babylon, if you like, and I will look after you; but if you do not want to, then don't come. Look, the whole country lies before you; go wherever you please." However, before Jeremiah turned to go, Nebuzaradan added, "Go back to Gedaliah son of Ahikam, the son of Shaphan, whom the king of Babylon has appointed over the towns of Judah, and live with him among the people, or go anywhere else you please." Then the commander gave him provisions and a present and let him go. So, Jeremiah went to Gedaliah son of Ahikam at Mizpah and stayed with him among the people who were left behind in the land.*

- Jeremiah is freed from captivity.
- The Babylonian commander recognizes who he is and treats him with respect. Jeremiah endured a lot of disrespect from the people when he spoke God's word. Jeremiah would not have expected any better from the Babylonians, but what he received here would have reminded him that God indeed sees all and has ways of providing in the most unexpected ways.
- Jeremiah is given a choice – a relatively attractive offer to go and live comfortably in Babylon because the captain of the guard would look after him. Those who were taken captive were compelled to go, they did not have a choice.
- Or he could go to Gedaliah – Gedaliah as it says in the verses above is the one, King Nebuchadnezzar appointed over the towns of Judah. That means that Jeremiah would again be well looked after.
- Or he could go anywhere he would please – For choices like this to be given, does it even sound like the Jeremiah belonged to the people who were taken captive by the Babylonians.
- And the Babylonian in addition gives him provisions and a present and sends Jeremiah.

The way Jeremiah was provided for was beyond what he would have imagined or anticipated. As Paul wrote to the church in Ephesus, ***Ephesians 3:20*** *"Now to him who is able to do immeasurably more than all we ask or imagine, according to his power that is at work within us."*

Self-Reflection: This story in scripture reminds us that in the midst of a trial when we feel God is far away, He is right there with you making a way for you. His provision can come through unexpected ways and through unexpected means. He is Lord of your hill tops and your valleys, cling to his faithfulness and trust in his word because God is sovereign, trustworthy, faithful and is working on your behalf - place your trust in him.

Prayer: Lord, thank you that you are God who is faithful, trustworthy and always cares. Help us to remember these truths and wait on your provision and care and not doubt you in the midst of our trials. Amen.

TRUSTWORTHY FATHER

 Discussion Questions

1. From the Scripture passages, contrast the difference in how Nebuchadnezzar instructs Jeremiah to be treated verses how he treated King Zedekiah and the officials. What could be the reason?
2. Where was Jeremiah when the Babylonian commander of the guard came looking for him, what do you think might have been going through Jeremiah's mind at the time?
3. What did Nebuzaradan understand about what had just transpired in Judah? Why do you think he could see something that God's people seemed not to?
4. What choices were given to Jeremiah about where he could live?
5. Where did Jeremiah choose to stay after he was freed by the Babylonians? Discuss what purpose God may have had in leading Jeremiah to this decision?
6. Why do we at times struggle to simply trust God? Does change affect our trust in God?
7. What is the difference between passive trust and active trust?

What promise of God will you retain in your mind as you dwell on the trustworthy nature of God?

LESSON 15

Willing to do God's Will

Would your faith and obedience to God ring hollow in light of your own desires?

 Scripture Passage: ***Jeremiah 42 and 43***

As the story continues after the fall of Jerusalem, those who were still in Jerusalem (called as the remnant), sought out Jeremiah.

They sought Jeremiah, not the other way around, the very same prophet of God whose words of warning they ignored – why did they do so? They were desperate, for what you may ask. They were desperate for God's favour.

They were seeking God's favour as they were afraid. All that Jeremiah prophesied came about. Their home was taken over by the Babylonians. The very foundation of their security as they perceived it, was eroded and so they turn in desperation to Jeremiah with a request.

Their request took the form of a prayer. Not one for forgiveness or safety, but a prayer with an inquiry to know God's will for their next steps.

"Pray that the Lord your God will tell us where we should go and what we should do." (Jeremiah 42:3)

Did they have any remorse to their neglect of God's word earlier, Scripture does not allude to them having any remorse but as the story unfolds it gives us insight to their hearts condition. And their reference to God as 'your God' when speaking to Jeremiah is quite telling of where their relationship with God was at the time.

Jeremiah says that he will certainly pray and tell all that the Lord instructs him to *(Jeremiah 42:4)*.

The people do not end their request there but continue to declare, *"May the Lord be a true and faithful witness against us if we do not act in accordance with everything the Lord your God sends you to tell us. Whether it is favourable or unfavourable, we will obey the Lord our God, to whom we are sending you, so that it will go well with us, for we will obey the Lord our God." (Jeremiah 42:5-6)*

Though they declare their desire to do God's will, they soon demonstrate that they had already decided to follow their own inclinations *(Jeremiah 43:2)*

Romans 8:31b says *"If God is for you, who can be against you."*

This verse alludes that God is most powerful, no opposition can successfully stand against, when God is with you. The people with confidence declare that God can be a witness against them if they do not obey, and in light of their failure to follow through with obedience in this instance, it implies a callousness in their understanding and regard for God.

Self-Reflection: We see a similar callousness exhibited in people's behaviour when God's grace, love and forgiveness are taken for granted. And along with an excuse that after all I am human and will falter, comes a justification to give into sinful desires, with no intentional steps towards changing sinful patterns, and thereby eclipsing for themselves the reality of a God who is Holy and also Just.

The Remnant of Judah further emphasise that God's will might be favourable or unfavourable, but they would still obey. The reason for this is stated in the verse, so that it may go well with them. Assumption that God may direct them contrary to what their heart desires, is good and wise and to that they reiterate that they will obey. And knowledge that their obedience matters for God's hand and favour to be upon them is evident. With their words they claim a surety of obedience from their end, but we see that it does not eventuate into action.

Self-Reflection: How would we react when our heart is set upon something and God's will for us is the exact opposite? Would our claims of faith and obedience ring hollow in light of our own desires?

God's will for them was to stay in Jerusalem; he promises to build them up, to keep them safe and to show compassion towards them and God specifies not only his will but the consequences of what would happen if they disobeyed and chose to go to Egypt.

Jeremiah 42:21-22 *"I(Jeremiah) have told you today, but you still have not obeyed the Lord your God in all he sent me to tell you. So now, be sure of this: You will die by the sword, famine and plague in the place where you want to go to settle."*

These words by Jeremiah were said at the end of speaking God's word to them. They have already not obeyed, when they were yet to respond to Jeremiah. We see their verbal response a few verses later at the start of the next chapter.

Before they could even respond, Jeremiah says that they already disobeyed? Why does he say so?

Jeremiah received the word from God ten days after the request from the people (Jeremiah 42:7). What did they do in those ten days? Did they act in manner that reflects a desire to honour and obey the word of God? Their actions during their waiting period would not have reflected a heart that was set to follow what God would say. It is interesting to note that the answer came ten days later to Jeremiah, it was like God knew and was testing their genuineness to obey him as they waited.

Self-Reflection: Take a moment and think back on when you sought God for direction or an answer to know what next, but while you waited, your actions were more reflective of what you set your heart to do rather than waiting on God?

From *Jeremiah 43:2* we see that when they hear that the word of God did not align with what they wanted, they immediately say, Jeremiah is lying. Reflecting on their response, it implies that their mind was set on going to Egypt and we can probably assume that their actions in the ten days of waiting reflected that.

What good is waiting without obedience to God. While we wait, we are to keep the way of God.

Psalm 37:34 says *"Hope in the Lord and keep his way. He will exalt you to inherit the land; when the wicked are destroyed, you will see it."*

The remnant of Judah placed their desires above God's, they wanted God's favour on their plan instead of heeding to God's plan for them. While they had to wait, they did not do so in obedience and submission to God, pressing into scriptures to keep their hope and trust firm without wavering.

John 5:19 says *"Jesus said to them, truly I say to you, the son can do nothing of his own accord, but only what he sees the Father doing. For whatever the Father does, the son does likewise."*

Jesus demonstrated obedience far beyond just words, his time as man evidenced a life of obedience to the Father that we strive to follow. We are to be obedient while we wait on God and even if in the moment God's will seems favourable or unfavourable, our obedience should not depend on it.

Prayer: Lord, we thank you that we can come to you with our concerns and know that you hear them and will answer them with your wisdom and in your timing. Often as we seek to hear from you, it involves a time of waiting, help us Lord during those times to not fall back on our commitment to be obedient to you but follow through with keeping your will and desires before our own. Amen.

Discussion Questions

1. What request do the remnant come to Jeremiah with and on the surface, how does this appeal look?
2. What was the message from the Lord? What does God want His people to do?
3. How did the people receive Jeremiah's words? What did they do? Is there any way they could have misunderstood God's instructions?
4. If we are going to seek God's plan, what do we need to believe about it?
5. Why does God sometimes require that we wait, and discuss how should we wait on God?

LESSON 16

Misplaced Trust

For our hearts to be aligned with God, our gaze has to be fixed on Him

 Scripture Passage: *Jeremiah 44*

As people we can be inclined to trust in our own capabilities, in systems placed in society for protection, in our finances or in our leaders. When we place our trust in anything or anyone other than God, it creates a distance between us and our creator. This eventuates into not being able to recognise when he speaks to us and blinds us to our own spiritual state.

In *Jeremiah 44,* we see the remnant of Judah who fled to Egypt, completely fail to recognise that their disobedience to God is what led them into the very situation they found themselves in. They attribute their good times prior to the downfall of Jerusalem to their worship of a pagan god – the queen of heaven. They had so distanced themselves from God through their sin and disobedience that they could no longer see the truth for what it was.

The chapter begins with Jeremiah sharing God's word to them. God in his mercy again reminds them of what truly led them to the situation they find themselves in, that the disaster brought on them was because of the evil they did *(verse 2-6)*. God speaks to them through Jeremiah, warning them that they would continue to have his anger brought upon them even in Egypt, if they persist in their sinful ways of idolatry. God is once again trying to reach and reason with them.

What do the remnant say in response to God's message?

Jeremiah 44:16-17a "We will not listen to the message you have spoken to us in the name of the Lord! We will certainly do everything we said we would: We will burn incense to the Queen of Heaven and will pour out drink offerings to her just as we and our ancestors, our kings and our officials did in the towns of Judah and in the streets of Jerusalem."

When we read these verses, it is difficult to comprehend why they remain stubborn in their disobedience to God. God had made it abundantly clear through his prophets that it was their idolatry, lack of reverence and obedience to him that brought upon the judgment they faced. Neither words nor seeing those prophesies coming true have managed to snap them out of their spiritual stupor.

We see their faulty reasoning in the following verses.

Jeremiah 44:17b-18 says *"At that time we had plenty of food and were well off and suffered no harm. But ever since we stopped burning incense to the Queen of Heaven and pouring out drink offerings to her, we have had nothing and have been perishing by sword and famine."*

A misplaced trust in an empty idol is what we see here. They were so far removed from God that they fail to see that the very actions they assumed kept them safe and in a time of abundance were what aroused God's anger.

To their response, Jeremiah says in verses 21-23 *"Did not the Lord remember and call to mind the incense burned in the towns of Judah and the streets of Jerusalem by you and your ancestors, your kings and your officials and the people of the land? When the Lord could no longer endure your wicked actions and the detestable things you did, your land became a curse and a desolate waste without inhabitants, as it is today. Because you have burned incense and have sinned against the Lord and have not obeyed him or followed his law or his decrees or his stipulations, this disaster has come upon you, as you now see."*

They completely miss the truth of their situation. God's blessings, his protection, mercy and patience that they experienced before he waited for them to turn back to him, seem completely missed by the people who were blinded by their own sin.

Self-Reflection: When consistently disobedient, our focus is turned away from God. And when our gaze is fixated elsewhere, our hearts are no more set on him but rather on what we have chosen to put in his place. Gradually there is a desensitisation to his works and recognition of his grace and mercy in our lives. This further hardens our hearts, leading to a stubbornness in our sinful ways. And our hearts become calibrated in such a way that stepping out of God's will no longer registers as wrong. For our hearts to be aligned with God's, our gaze has to always remain on him. If not, there comes a definite lack of spiritual discernment along with a misplaced trust in something or someone else other than God.

Jeremiah's message to the people fell on deaf ears. As Jesus often said *"Those who have ears let them hear."* He refers to spiritual ears, a discernment that comes with the presence of the spirit within us.

1 Corinthians 2:14 says *"The person without the Spirit does not accept the things that come from the Spirit of God but considers them foolishness, and cannot understand them because they are discerned only through the Spirit."*

MISPLACED TRUST

When one is unable to perceive God's workings or understand his message, it is called spiritual blindness. The heart of spiritual discernment is knowing and recognising God's voice and his workings from those of the world's.

Acts 28:26-27 says *"Go to this people and say, "You will be ever hearing but never understanding; you will be ever seeing but never perceiving." For this people's heart has become calloused; they hardly hear with their ears, and they have closed their eyes."*

Self-Reflection: We can be inclined to glory in our achievements, trust in futile things and Satan revels when we do it, but as my friend says "Walking with the Holy Spirit helps us to have discernment. He will guide us along the rocky path of life. When we stay anchored to the Lord each day, we will not be led astray."

1 Corinthians 1:18 says *"For the message of the cross is foolishness to those who are perishing, but to us who are being saved, it is the power of God."*

The word of God was foolishness to the remnant in Egypt, but let's remember those like Daniel and his friends Shadrach, Meshack and Abednego who were taken captive to Babylon, the word of God was power to them. Their faith in God never faltered, their trust never wavered and their gaze never scattered.

Prayer: Lord, forgive us when we are stubborn. Help us stay close to you and prevent us from failing to recognise your hand and your workings in our life. Give us discernment to recognise them and if we do step out of your path, help us to realign ourselves to you. Lord, keep us close to you and sheltered under your wings. Amen.

Discussion Questions

1. What does Jeremiah have to remind the people of Judah of in chapter 44:1-10 and why does he have to do that?
2. What do the remnant say in response to God's message?
3. What led the people to reach a place of lack in discerning their ways? How can we guard ourselves from ever seeing but never understanding?
4. Discuss what is spiritual discernment? Why is it essential?

What are some of the ways we can grow in discernment?

LESSON 17

Being Faithful in a Fragmented World

"His Lord said to Him, well done, good and faithful servant"
Matthew 25:21a

 Scripture Passage: *Jeremiah 45*

Jeremiah 45 entails a message of encouragement to Baruch from God.

Who was Baruch?

Baruch was Jeremiah's faithful scribe and friend. Baruch was obedient to God and was beside Jeremiah through his ministry. Baruch wrote all the words God instructed Jeremiah to in a scroll and even at times spoke on Jeremiah's behalf as we see in *Jer 36:10*.

Because of Baruch's faithfulness and obedience to God, he along with Jeremiah were sought after by King Jehoiakim. Baruch too shared Jeremiah's anguish of finding themselves in challenging circumstances because of their faithfulness to God.

Baruch's words to God

Jeremiah 45:2-3 *This is what the Lord, the God of Israel, says to you, Baruch: You said, 'Woe to me! The Lord has added sorrow to my pain; I am worn out with groaning and find no rest."*

These words give us a glimpse into the heaviness in Baruch's heart. It implies a weariness that seeped deeper than just physical tiredness but more so seemed to stem from being emotionally drained. But within that cry to God is also a very self-focused complaint. Baruch's cry is 'Me' focused. He says Woe to me! My pain, I am worn out and find no rest. He also states that the Lord is the one further adding to his anguish.

Self-Reflection: There is no fault in pouring our hearts out to God when we struggle with something, but God does not want us to have a skewed view of him by remaining in our lament.

He had a word for his weary servant, and he wanted Baruch to view things through a different lens.

God's words to Baruch

Jeremiah 45:4-5 outlines God's message to Baruch through Jeremiah *"But the Lord has told me to say to you, 'This is what the Lord says: I will overthrow what I have built and uproot what I have planted, throughout the earth. Should you then seek great things for yourself? Do not seek them. For I will bring disaster on all people, declares the Lord, but wherever you go I will let you escape with your life.'"*

As Baruch stood alongside Jeremiah and kept on hearing the words of judgement for the disobedient people of Judah, the impending doom was eventually what Baruch might have begun to focus more on. And that would have sat heavy on his heart making him focus on the bleak future that lay ahead for him.

Self-Reflection: How often do we narrow our vision to all that seems to be going wrong around us? And just like Baruch, even though we are filled with the knowledge that God is with us, it can be hard to not let the messes in front of and around us chip away at our perspective on things.

God is Sovereign and Almighty

The Lord begins with reminding Baruch of his sovereign power. Either being in difficult situations ourselves or being a part of a world that seems stubborn in not recognising their need for God can often leave one with a feeling of helplessness making one woeful of all that is happening. But just as God reminded Baruch that he is the one who builds and uproots throughout the earth, it is a reminder for us too that however removed from God things might seem to us, they are never out of his watchful eye, his sovereign will and his control.

What are you seeking?

God points to the futility of seeking seemingly great things through his words to Baruch of the surety of overthrow and uprooting of the nation of Judah. The seemingly great things that God refers to are those that have mere earthly value, that which perishes with our time here in the world.

💭 *Self-Reflection:* What are the seemingly great things that we might have set our hearts on and are seeking after? Are we rightfully valuing the things of God above our earthly pursuits?

Baruch was the son of Neriah. In *Jer 51:59* we read of another son of Neriah, Seraiah, who is described as a staff officer of king Zedekiah. In the eyes of the world, between the two brothers, Seraiah had the position, the comfort and the acceptance of the people. But Baruch pursued the things of God rather than the things of this world. In his moments of glum ponderings, Baruch might have been prone to compare his situation with his brother's. Hence the Lord reminds him to recalibrate himself and set his heart's desires on what he should really be seeking after. God's direction to Baruch is clear when he says to him, *"Seek them not"*

God's words are a reminder to Baruch to shift his focus back on God, and on God's call and purpose on his life. May this be a reminder for us too, to reflect on what we are seeking after. Trust the Lord, let him be the centre of your world.

And God ends his message to Baruch with a promise of protection. Baruch would face hardships, but he would always have God with him. A precious reminder for us that we will never be without God and that is the greatest assurance we can have.

To stand for the things of God with conviction, consistency and faithfulness in the midst of a people who were stubborn in their sin and refused to repent, was a call God placed on Jeremiah's and Baruch's life. When we read through Jeremiah, we harbor a very lonely road for him on his God given path but knowing that Baruch, his scribe and friend was beside him reminds us that God in a way did provide that support for both of them through that friendship. That does not negate one's dependence on

God but it sure does make walking the narrow road a little bit easier. They shared a bond of faithfulness to God.

Self-Reflection: For many of us we may not be called to be walking like Jeremiah in the front and centre on a public platform. But like Baruch we can be faithful friends and supporters to each other as we walk the narrow path, pursuing the things of God, living out his plan and purpose for our lives and being faithful to the Almighty.

Prayer: Lord, as we walk in the path you have chosen for us, at times it is lonely, at times it is hard and many a times it is wearisome. In those moments, may we turn to you and seek comfort but also have our eyes opened to having the right perspective of what truly matters. Help us to not give up on doing good. We thank you for those in Christ who walk alongside us, encourage and pour into us. May we do the same for them too. Help us Lord to remain faithful to you in this fragmented world. Amen.

Discussion Questions

1. What did Baruch complain to God about? Discuss God's response to Baruch.
2. God's response reminds us to reflect on the things we have set our hearts on. How do we balance out living a good life vs not letting temporal things become more important than spiritual things?
3. Baruch felt dissatisfied with his situation. What are some of the common reasons dissatisfaction creeps into our hearts?
4. "For I have learned in whatever situation I am to be content" *(Philippian 4:11)*. What made Paul's contentment possible? How does Paul's view of contentment compare with the world's view of contentment?
5. Why does God want his children to be content? What is he trying to teach us?
6. "Godliness with contentment is great gain" *(1 Timothy 6:6)*. How does godliness relate to contentment? What are some ways we can strive for godliness?
7. What do you think is 'the great gain' in godliness with contentment?

LESSON 18

The Narrow Path

"Enter through the narrow gate. For wide is the gate and broad is the road to destruction, and many enter through it. But small is the gate and narrow is the road that leads to life, and only a few find it."
Matthew 7:13-14

 Scripture Passage: **Jeremiah 46-52**

With this lesson, we come to a close of our study through Jeremiah. Through this lesson, we will touch upon themes that are specific to the relevant scripture passages mentioned above, and a couple of general takeaways from our study.

Jeremiah lived in days that echo our times today in many ways. Wickedness, corruption, false teaching, disrespect for God, disregard for his word and his ways, pursuit of self and satisfaction outside of God. The last few chapters of Jeremiah (46-52), consist of a series of prophecies against nations, it begins with Egypt and ends with Babylon, the two main powers that vied for control of Judah during Jeremiah's time.

Pursuit

Throughout the book of Jeremiah, the pursuit of God's people by God himself was evident. He is a God who is faithful and does not forsake those who are his. What did the people pursue? Their pursuit was more fleshly, false gods, and idols took centre stage with emphasis on gratifying their own desires.

Self-Reflection: What are we pursuing? Is there a pursuit of God in our lives? If so, what does it look like today? Is the pursuit of God our priority, is it dictated by how we feel, our circumstances or any other distractions? Is our pursuit the glory of God or do we place self before God?

Deception

Jeremiah 9:6 says "You live in the midst of deception. In their deceit they refuse to acknowledge me."

The things of this world can mislead, our hearts can deceive. What opens our eyes to the Truth? Only the Spirit can. God opens our spiritual eyes and ears to see and understand the things of God. The people of Judah saw and heard but they did not understand. They knew of God, but what came of that knowledge?

Awareness and knowledge have two very different meanings. Being aware of the word and the works of God is not the same as *knowing* God. Even the demons know who God is *(James 2:19)*. Knowing God is to seek him and have a daily and active relationship with him. And knowing him should rightfully impact how we live, for HIM.

Self-Reflection: Has your knowledge of God seeped in from your head to your heart?

Have you moved from knowing of him to seeking, pursuing and knowing him?

And how has that impacted the way you do everyday life?

Security

In the last few chapters of Jeremiah, we read of messages that describe the destruction that those nations will face at the hand of God, Egypt (ch 46), Philistines (ch 47), Moab (ch 48), Ammon, Edom, Damascus (ch 49) and Babylon (ch 50-51).

These nations relied on their own military prowess. They seemed strong, stable, powerful and would have been tempting for the people of Judah to seek refuge in.

Jeremiah 46:10 says "But that day belongs to the Lord, the Lord Almighty-a day of vengeance, for vengeance on His foes."

God's words point to his Sovereignty. God's sovereignty extends to all nations, all will be held accountable before him. He did not want the people to seek refuge in any other nation, they were to trust him and seek refuge in him.

Self-Reflection: What are we finding our security in? When circumstances feel less than ideal who or what do we seek refuge in? Does your trust rest in God or do you tend to be tossed by the waves of your turmoil?

God's love endures forever

Jeremiah 46: 28 "Do not fear, O Jacob my servant, for I am with you, declares the Lord. Though I completely destroy all the nations among which I scatter you, I will not completely destroy you. I will discipline you but only with justice; I will not let you go entirely unpunished."

God speaks with clarity to remind the people that even though they were under his discipline, he would never forsake them.

Self-Reflection: Even though God's people rebelled and lived in the consequences of their disobedience, God remained faithful. If you have ever turned from God, disregarded his warnings or call, know that he never gives up on you. It is never too late to surrender to him. He welcomes all those who come to him with a humble and repentant heart. He is patiently and faithfully waiting for you to turn to him.

The Narrow Path

The prophet Jeremiah teaches us obedience in the face of adversity, and faithfulness to God in a fragmented world. He was reluctant to be a prophet at the beginning to a people who were not for God. He endured physical and emotional struggles as he stayed obedient to God. There were times when Jeremiah wanted to give up.

Jeremiah reminds us that to walk the narrow path may not be easy but as we walk on the narrow path often our gaze gets pulled to the challenges and contention the world we live in has with followers of Christ. But as we walk, may we always remind ourselves that although the path is narrow and challenging, where it leads to is what matters, and that is to God. One day in his courts is better than a thousand elsewhere *(Psalm 84:10.)*

Matthew 10:25 says *"It is enough for the disciple that he be as his master, and the servant as his lord."*

Self-Reflection: Is it enough for us to be like our master, Jesus? He followed the will of God to the cross, he humbly washed the disciple's feet, he came as man for our sake, going to the poor, needy and the outcast, being rejected and despised, not receiving the approval or applause of man.

And as Jeremiah walked in his calling, reflect on whether you are willing to walk and work for the kingdom of God without the accolades and the applause?

The book of Jeremiah also reminds us of the promise of God with us, carrying us through the call he places on our lives. Even when not easy, there is a joy to be found in walking in obedience to God.

> In obedience help me walk, the narrow path leading to thee
> The world and its distractions trying to sink its talons in me
> Hide me under your wings, for it is in you Lord I seek to be
> My heart and my mind are yours to have
> I claim no ownership of them you see
> For when in you Lord, I am rightfully where I belong to be.
> *Manu David*

<u>Discussion Questions</u>

1. In Ch 46-52, we see a series of prophesies against all the nations that vied for control of Judah. What do you learn/understand from the fact that all the nations would drink the cup of God's wrath as their punishment?
2. As we conclude our study series on Jeremiah, take some time and reflect on the lessons you have learnt and share anything new you learnt, truths you have been reminded of and anything that has impacted you.